Ten Ways
THE CHURCH
Has Changed

Ten Ways
THE CHURCH
Has Changed

What history can teach us
about uncertain times

Christopher M. Bellitto, Ph.D.

Pauline
BOOKS & MEDIA
Boston

Library of Congress Cataloging-in-Publication Data

Bellitto, Christopher M.

Ten ways the church has changed : what history can teach us about uncertain times/ Christopher M. Bellitto.— 1st ed.

    p. cm.

Includes bibliographical references and index.

ISBN 0-8198-7418-3 (pbk.)

1. Catholic Church—History. I. Title.

BX945.3.B45 2006

282.09—dc22

     2005028066

The Scripture quotations contained herein are from the *New Revised Standard Version Bible: Catholic Edition*, copyright © 1989, 1993, Division of Christian Education of the National Council of the Churches of Christ in the United States of America. Used by permission. All rights reserved.

Cover design by Rosana Usselmann

Cover photo and insides Sami Sarkis/Getty Images

"P" and PAULINE are registered trademarks of the Daughters of St. Paul.

Published by Pauline Books & Media, 50 Saint Paul's Avenue, Boston, MA 02130-3491. www.pauline.org

Printed in the U.S.A.

Pauline Books & Media is the publishing house of the Daughters of St. Paul, an international congregation of women religious serving the Church with the communications media.

1 2 3 4 5 6 7 8 9 10   11 10 09 08 07 06

For Bob and Katherine Engelhardt
my parents (in-law) and my friends

CONTENTS

ACKNOWLEDGMENTS

I AM GRATEFUL to those who helped me with this project: Anthony J. Bellitto Jr., Rev. Francis J. Corry, and Sr. Janet Baxendale, S.C., read the manuscript in whole or part, offering advice and suggestions. At Pauline Books & Media, I thank Sr. Marianne Lorraine, FSP, Sr. Kathryn James, FSP, and Sr. Bernadette M. Reis, FSP, for first suggesting this project and then reworking its form (in print and online) several times as it developed. I am especially happy to have had Sr. Lorraine's encouragement, perspective, and feedback as I worked through the text. My classroom students and the audience members at public lectures offered many questions, challenges, and comments that worked their way into my thinking. I, of course, am solely responsible for the final decisions and analyses that ended up in this book, but I remain humbled by the patience, generosity of spirit, and efforts of all of these people on my behalf. Finally, and as always, I thank Karen Bellitto, my wife and my best friend, for being her and for helping me to be me.

PROLOGUE

THE BOOK YOU HOLD in your hands is not a complete history of the Church. Its goal is more modest: to demonstrate how the Church, over the course of two thousand years, has adapted to changing circumstances while staying true to her core principles. There has been much talk since Vatican II (1962–1965) that the Church has to change in order to keep up-to-date. As the Council documents say, the Church must read the signs of the times and make sure she is actively engaged with the world. At the same time, however, the Church is not going to give up what makes the Church the Church: she is not going to change doctrine because a particular belief is no longer fashionable. What she can do—and, in fact, as this book hopes to demonstrate—what she has done many times over two millennia, is to alter the way she communicates those doctrines and to adapt religious practices to the diverse cultures in which she lives.

Does this mean the Church changes? The answer is: yes and no. Change is not new in Church history; it didn't start with Vatican II. Indeed, when you study the history of the Church, you are struck by the constant change and development that occurred. Why? It's important to remember that no catechism, code of canon law, complete Bible, or list of seven sacraments came flying down from heaven after Jesus returned to his Father on the Ascension. Statements of what the Church teaches and how she will celebrate her faith and beliefs took time to come into being.

However, let me immediately clarify an important point: doctrine doesn't change, but the way we explain doctrine does. At the same time, discipline—meaning loosely how the Church is run, what her rules are, and the manner in which we exercise our faith—can indeed change. To put it another way: divine law doesn't change, but human law changes very frequently. The challenge is to know the difference and to make sure that change and development begin from real roots and grow organically, authentically, and within the appropriate authority system.

This book is the story of ten of those challenges. As you read, I suggest that you take particular note of how things develop and change: what can and can't change, what does and doesn't change, what should and should not change, the pace of change, whether change happened too quickly or slowly, whether change was explained well or not, and above all how the subjects of these ten lessons were adapted to different times, places, cultures, and peoples.

I have made this book user-friendly in two central ways. The first is by selecting ten stories or lessons that I believe illustrate this principle of balanced, authentic change. These ten areas are not the only things that have changed in Church history, but they make the case as well as any others. These ten stories—individually and as a group—also allow us to see Church history from several angles: from the top of the hierarchy, the grass roots Church in the pews, and the several layers in between.

The second way I have made the book user-friendly is to divide Church history into six ages. Previously, a famous Church historian named Christopher Dawson did the same thing, building on biblical, ancient, and medieval notions that there are six ages of human existence. But my six ages do not precisely match Dawson's or the various conceptions of time offered by other Church historians and theologians. The six ages that I selected when planning this book make sense to me as a teacher, writer, and public lecturer. I think, too, that they will help guide this study of change.

EARLY CA. 30–461, Jesus to the end of Leo I's papacy
FIRST MILLENNIUM 461–1073, Leo I to the end of Gregory VII's papacy
MEDIEVAL 1073–1467, Gregory VII to Erasmus' birth
REFORMATION 1467–1648, Erasmus to the end of the Thirty Years' War
EARLY MODERN 1648–1848, Thirty Years' War to Europe's "Year of Revolutions"
MODERN 1848–TODAY, "Year of Revolutions" to Vatican II and beyond

This division of ages is not always precise, I admit. What I call the first millennium Church, for example, starts not with Jesus' birth but after the reign of Leo I (the Great) in 461. The first four centuries of the Church's life are chronologically part of the first millennium. But this division indicates that the Church between the fall of the Roman Empire and the early Middle Ages was a unique era. While some big names and events serve as guideposts-popes and wars, for example-the story told in this book is neither exclusively top-down history (the "Great Man" theory) nor bottom-up history (the people in the pews), but an attempt to marry both perspectives.

These ten lessons can be read in whole, in part, and in any order. Some material naturally overlaps, for no matter how anyone divides Church history into eras and themes, it is impossible to separate them entirely. Particularly illustrative examples of how Christianity encountered paganism in the first millennium appear several times. Erasmus, Luther, and the Enlightenment must constantly reappear, as well. This overlap functions not as repetition, but as glue.

Finally, while the first three ages of each of the ten lessons largely deal with the Mediterranean world and Europe, as they must, I tried to look beyond Europe after Columbus' first voyage in 1492. When Christianity reaches America in the early modern centuries, I used American examples to round out the story. Moreover, we are only now, at the dawn of the third millennium, beginning to appreciate global Catholicism. The full impact of that story must be left to future Church historians. For now, however, let us turn to the Church's past in order to understand and gain perspective on her present.

Chapter 1

ORGANIZATION

*How was the Church organized
and governed?*

The Early Church: Local Leadership

THE QUESTION OF HOW THE CHURCH is organized and governed relates to the branch of theology known as ecclesiology: the nature, structure, and function of the Church. Throughout this section, therefore, we will repeatedly meet the question of who is in charge of the Church, which naturally can lead to conflicting interpretations. To begin, when we think about the early Church, today's model has to be the furthest thing from our minds. There was no centralized papacy in the first centuries after Jesus, but rather a series of local churches, each of which gradually came to be led by one bishop. Perhaps the best image is that of a chain of islands—an archipelago of Christian communities spread across the Mediterranean shores—each of which was generally independent, but often in contact with others. The communities sent letters of encouragement and questions to each other. When Christians traveled, they surely sought out other Christians in the towns they visited, if only for safety since Christianity was still an underground, illegal religion before the early fourth century.

In this context, then, several developments occurred slowly. The first concerned the organization of the new Christians. Since the first Christians were Jews, it was natural to adapt the synagogue's model of elders, readers, and those who cared for the material needs of the congregation. For a time, the word synagogue ("gathering") was used alongside *ekklesia* ("church" or "assembly"). As Christianity moved away from Judaism, particular Christian offices emerged: bishops, priests, and deacons—who were sometimes grouped together as "elders"—and then lectors, catechists, and others. Elders were sometimes called by the Latin word *saniores* (the older or wiser ones) and appear to have originally been lay leaders who oversaw the Christian community. After the third century, as orders and ordination began to develop more formally, this category of "elders" dropped away.

The second development was monepiscopacy: each community gathered under the leadership and direction of one man, the local bishop, who personified the community. During the sporadic persecutions by the Roman Empire's authorities, often the bishop was killed in the hope that the community would be, in a sense, decapitated. But Christianity continued to grow, to the Romans' disappointment and amazement. The bishop (*episkopos,* borrowing the word for a supervisor or inspector) traced his heritage and authority to the original apostles.

The local bishop played several roles: he was an administrative leader, chief preacher, judge, and central liturgical celebrant. We hear of the bishop's importance in a letter written by Ignatius, the bishop of Antioch, who was martyred in Rome's Colosseum around 110–117. Writing to the Christian community in Smyrna, he advised: "Apart from the bishop let no one do anything pertaining to the Church," adding a moment later, "let the people be present wherever the bishop appears, just as the Catholic Church is wherever Jesus Christ is."[1] In each community, one liturgy was celebrated each Sunday, further linking the bishop with the Eucharist as the unifying center of the Church's body.

Did this mean bishops were all on an equal footing and did not come under other bishops? The answer depends, essentially, on whom you asked. This aspect of Church organization was worked out, sometimes contentiously, in these first centuries. For Cyprian, the bishop of Carthage in North Africa who died as a martyr in 258, the episcopacy "is one, of which each [bishop] holds his part in its totality." Cyprian considered the bishop of Rome to be the "source of the episcopacy" because of Peter's designation by Christ as the origin of unity. But, for Cyprian, "other apostles were also the same as was Peter, endowed with an equal partnership both of honor and of power, but the beginning proceeds from unity so that the Church of Christ may be shown to be one."[2]

Cyprian was not always so diplomatic. In 256, he led a council in North Africa that challenged Stephen I, the bishop of Rome (254–257). There, Cyprian stressed that Peter had not claimed supremacy over Paul nor required his obedience. Cyprian complained, "For no one of us sets himself up as a bishop of bishops nor by autocratic intimidation compels his colleagues to a forced obedience." This council asserted that the Roman bishop could confirm their decisions on appeal, but he could not reverse them. Intervention was certainly not welcome, and we see this in the language of the bishops' letters. Many bishops addressed each other—including the bishops of Rome—as "brother," but Damasus I (366–384) of Rome called bishops his "sons."

A third development occurred in Rome that both complemented and challenged monepiscopacy in the Christian archipelago. There was a sense that Peter's mandate from Christ and his presence in the empire's capital gave that city a special role. It was not uncommon for Christian bishops outside Rome to disagree with the bishop of Rome in this period, as Cyprian did. But the bishop of Rome was steadily developing a more central and dominating role. Supporters of Roman authority stated that a bishop's power of the keys passed through Rome, just as Peter passed the authority that Christ had given to him along to the other apostles. This argument said that, while local bishops have pastoral responsibility for their part of the Church, it is the bishop of Rome who has the ultimate and full pastoral responsibility for the entire Church. The local bishop only shares in that fullness of power partly and locally.

A fourth development linked these others. As the Church grew larger and more extensive geographically, a system of organization naturally emerged. This was modeled on that of the Roman Empire's structures and grew gradually. A metropolitan bishop was one put in charge of a local city and its surrounding district. Bishops of larger cities oversaw metropolitans; the most famous of these early ones are Rome, Carthage, Alexandria, Antioch, and Ephesus. Four hundred years after Jesus' resurrection, then, Christianity had clearly come far from a small group of unorganized followers on the edge of the Roman Empire.

The First Millennium Church:
Parishes and Dioceses

With the collapse of the Roman Empire in the West in the fifth century, the cities of Europe declined and the population moved into the countryside. Christianity's leaders, the bishops, moved into the civil leadership positions left by the Roman city officials, while parishes also grew in rural areas. Christianity grew and expanded at this time. But because of the empire's fall, communication slowed down and coordination among Christian communities declined. In a sense, the archipelago had expanded, but also grew further apart. To the Church's advantage, the old Roman system was already in place. Into its power vacuum walked the Church and in particular her bishops. They adopted much from the empire: Roman law systems, the Roman *lingua franca* of Latin as the official Church language, and Roman organization to administer a faith that would soon dominate Europe.

Christianity had first spread in the cities, and a *paganus* was a person from the countryside who had not heard of Jesus. Before the word "diocese" was applied to a city and its suburbs, it had first meant a neighborhood parish. In the first millennium, however, Christianity moved to the fields and forests. Rural parishes often grew up in the wake of a kind of preaching tour or evangelizing mission by bishops or missionary monks. These rural villages were small and far apart, so each needed a priest and Christian community. The rural parishes took root and spread in the sixth century. The word for village, *vicus,* eventually led to the idea of a vicar as someone who is in charge of a parish (though today it is often used for a priest who oversees a group of parishes).

As Europe organized itself in a feudal system of large landowners contracting with tenant farmers, the Roman imperial system broke down even further. Priests and parishes in the country grew distant from their urban bishops, with consequences that could damage the Church's independence. Each city retained the ancient model of only one bishop. But because dioceses had now grown very large, the need also grew for more parishes, more priests, and therefore more Masses on Sundays. Gone were the days of one liturgy with all the clergy and people gathered around the bishop. This growth was a blessing for the Church, but it added to the need for supervision and organized growth. A large landowner might build his own church or chapel on his land, a proprietary church as it was known, and decide that since he built the church, he could name the priest and control the Christian community. This arrangement challenged the Church's organization as well as its freedom, let alone the integrity of the sacraments, since a priest in such circumstances may not have been properly educated or examined by a bishop.

Christian life in the parish experienced an upsurge in liveliness and quality control in the eighth century, under Charlemagne (742–814). His goal—and the goal of the popes with whom he shared a close relationship as partner and patron—was to bring parishes more directly under the direction of bishops. The Church was trying to balance the independence of the local

Christian community with the necessary oversight of the bishop and, ultimately, the pope. At the same time, the Church did not want to offend the landowners, who supported the parish even while they threatened the local bishop's authority and jurisdiction.

The Church had to find a middle road. A system developed whereby a bishop would provide the priests with some of their income, while the landowner also supported the priests and the parishes. A tithing system was put in place. Although it had only partial success, it tried to allocate about three-quarters of the money collected in a parish for the needs of the parish and the priest. This included material needs, upkeep, and local charity. A quarter would go to the bishop. This system worked relatively well for a few decades, but with the death of Charlemagne's son Louis the Pious in 840, the plan fell apart along with the rest of Charlemagne's empire. As a result, many organizational problems followed: married clergy, inheritances, corruption, civil interference, and the question of just who pays the priest.

As these organizational developments and problems occurred on the local level, the Church took steps to organize herself on a higher and larger scale. Metropolitan bishops now came to be called archbishops, and bishops below them were suffragan bishops who came under the archbishops' authority, supervision, and jurisdiction. This system ensured that conflicts, questions, and appeals could be pursued in an orderly and fair manner up the hierarchical chain of authority. Once more, Christianity filled in the Roman Empire's structure. Just as Roman dioceses became

Christian dioceses (first as neighborhoods and then as larger regions), the boundaries of the Roman provinces were roughly followed as the archbishops' provinces or spheres of authority. An archbishop, therefore, came to be the bishop of the major provincial cities under the previous Roman Empire. Provinces, in turn, were grouped into even larger regions.

The homes of the archbishops were now growing dominant as powerful theological centers away from but in communion with Rome. The archbishop presided at the consecration of suffragan bishops and supervised local and regional synods and councils. By the ninth century, the archbishops exercised supreme power and prerogatives, at least in their own regions. They could settle disputed elections of bishops and abbots; they increased their juridical rights by hearing appeals in disputed cases of both civil and canon law, and they could buy and sell property without Roman approval. These cases sometimes resulted in conflicts between archbishops and their suffragan bishops. This in turn increased the prestige of the papacy as the ultimate court of appeal, therefore supporting the further development of the Church's hierarchical organization. All of this would explode in the Middle Ages.

The Medieval Church: Councils and Centralization

THE MIDDLE AGES WITNESSED two strongly opposed movements in the Church's development of her organizations. At the same time that the papacy was strengthening her structures by centralizing papal authority, general councils were arguing—in the most extreme case—that a council and not a pope was the ultimate authority in the Church. The very organizing and unifying principle of the Church's structural life was at stake.

The medieval papacy took a series of steps to consolidate its authority and power versus secular governments. At the same time, the popes made sure that they were seen as the ultimate executive, legislative, and judicial authorities within the body of the Church. This strikes American ears as odd, given not only the separation of church and state, but also the separation of powers in addition to checks and balances, which are ingrained in modern constitutional governments.

Meanwhile, proponents of general councils were promoting the idea that the pope is a kind of delegated administrator and the people of God are the ultimate authority in the Church. This, in turn, was based on an ecclesiology that said the Church was the mystical body of Christ (to use Paul's image in Corinthians). Practically speaking—to put it in less theological and more modern political terms—the people of God did not abdicate their sovereignty to the pope, but looked to him (and to their bishops) to exercise leadership in their name while always being accountable to the people. On another level, since everyone could not participate in Church matters, some type of representative institution must voice the people's concerns in an orderly and efficient manner. This led to the upsurge in "conciliarism"; there were several branches of conciliarism, with varying exercises of authority assigned to the pope. The fundamental questions ran on several levels of authority that had to be balanced: the bishop of Rome as the successor to Peter, the bishops of other places as successors to the apostles, the College of Cardinals, and the councils that helped run the Church since her first centuries. The goal was somehow to balance the singular authority of the pope with the corporate nature of the Church as the mystical body of Christ: many members gathered around and unified by the Eucharist.

Obviously, there is a crossover here with some emerging secular developments, such as the Magna Carta (1215), which talked about trials by jury, due process, and a king bound by the consent of those he governed. Parliaments in England were developing in such a way as to challenge royal authority, and the same was true of representative institutions throughout Europe, with different degrees of success. In Italy, especially, city-states and communes experimented with representative governments. However, the Church also had a long history of representation and participation. For centuries, monks and nuns had made decisions together in their monasteries and convents, even up to the point of electing their own abbots and abbesses. Religious orders like the Dominicans had done the same since the early thirteenth century. In some cities, priests elected their own bishops, as cardinals elected the popes.

Conciliar activity and authority was not a medieval innovation or heresy, therefore. Throughout the first thousand years of the Church, councils on the local, regional, and universal levels had met to consider the great theological and disciplinary questions of the day.

The earliest—Nicaea in 325—was called not by a pope but by the Emperor Constantine, yet its creed set the standard for what Christians say they believe about Jesus. Other general councils had little or no papal participation, although popes gradually played a larger role in the eight ecumenical councils that met in the first millennium. Very early in the process, it became the norm that popes had to confirm the councils' statements in order for these to be considered valid.

What changed in the Middle Ages was that popes tried to control the general councils: indeed, four Lateran councils met in the pope's own palace in Rome in 1123, 1139, 1179, and 1215. These were very papal events, but when the papacy began to lose its moral authority and become bogged down in pomp and politics, general councils stepped in to claim increased authority. The crisis came during the Great Western Schism (1378–1417) when two and then three popes (and subsequently two and then three colleges of cardinals) simultaneously competed for power.

Into this debate stepped the General Council of Constance (1414–1418), which continued to meet even after the pope who called it ran away in the middle of the night when it became clear he would be deposed by the general council's representatives. In April 1415, Constance declared that the highest authority in the Church is a general council:

> This holy synod of Constance...declares that, legitimately assembled in the Holy Spirit, constituting a general council and representing the Catholic Church militant, it has power immediately from Christ; and that everyone

of whatever state or dignity, even papal, is bound to obey it in those matters which pertain to the faith, the eradication of the said schism, and the general reform of the said Church of God in head and members.

How authoritative this statement is remains a matter of contention. The most mainstream analysis concludes that Constance had to make this statement and act to unify the papacy because of the extraordinary circumstances of the schism. In essence, this interpretation sees this statement of conciliar authority as a non-binding, once-in-a-lifetime situation that did not prejudice papal authority (although other interpretations see this statement as true: a general council is more powerful than the pope).

After deposing two of the three popes and forcing the third to resign, Constance oversaw the selection of a unifying pope, Martin V (1417–1431). He was elected by a one-time only extension of voting beyond the usual Colleges of Cardinals to include conciliar representatives. Before adjourning, Constance tried to make general councils a regular and not extraordinary feature of the Church's life. A decree named *Frequens* stated that a general council must meet frequently: once every ten years. For the next three decades, popes fought with general councils and these assertions. A series of strong popes eventually fought back the conciliar challenge, with the result that Pope Pius II (ironically, a former conciliarist) in 1460 condemned conciliarism as "erroneous and abominable."

By the end of the Middle Ages, then, the papacy was once more reasserting its ultimate authority, although it was yet again damaging itself with political patronage and secular matters. Conciliarism struggled to reassert itself, but by the time the next general council met, at Trent (1545–1563), it was clearly a council of bishops under the pope's leadership, whose decisions had to be approved and promulgated by the pope, otherwise they would have had no authority whatsoever. But these same bishops threw their efforts into revitalizing the Church at its basic level, in parishes, and that is where they made their stand in helping the Church recover from the conciliar and Protestant challenges.

The Reformation Church: Competing Ecclesiologies

ANY DISCUSSION OF HOW THE CHURCH during the Reformations considered the question of ecclesiology and of how the Church should be organized and governed must take into account the competing Protestant ecclesiologies. The Protestants sought to return the Church to its earliest models of decentralization, to greater participation by the laity, and (for those Protestant churches with bishops) to a role for the bishop that was fairly independent—and certainly not under the authority of a pope. Catholics responded to the Protestant challenges by reasserting very strongly the necessity and legitimacy of the episcopacy and especially the papacy. As a result, the idea of the Church as the mystical body of Christ was left back in the Middle Ages with the now largely defeated conciliarists.

After the Council of Trent, great efforts were put into centralization in Rome. During these centuries, the Church was organized and governed under the leadership of Rome, though local bishops and parishes played a very lively role, too, albeit not independently. The year after Trent adjourned in 1563, Rome issued a new *Index of Forbidden Books* as well as a Profession of Faith that embodied the careful doctrinal language Trent had worked out to restate the faith in light of the Protestant challenges. A few years later, an official catechism was published to teach this faith. This Roman catechism was soon followed by a new breviary (the book of daily prayers for the clergy) and then a missal and book of rites that guided the celebration of sacraments, especially the Eucharist at Mass.

To oversee this centralization, the popes in this period were selected for their administrative skills: most had canon law backgrounds and few had advanced training in theology. They emphasized their roles as absolute monarchs of the papal states, that is, as temporal rulers. When they turned their attention to spiritual matters, they took a more administrative and less pastoral approach as well. They were not, however, the scandalous Renaissance popes of the prior generation. Indeed, they were largely successful in their attempts at reorganizing the Church.

The best example of these attempts, from the very top of the Church, came under Pope Sixtus V (1585–1590), who in 1588 reorganized the papal bureaucracy—the curia—into fifteen congregations. Six congregations dealt with the temporal life of the

Church, which chiefly meant the papal states. These congregations administered food supplies, the navy (to defend the Italian coast from pirates), tax relief (what we might call a welfare system), universities, infrastructures, and legal matters. Another nine congregations focused on spiritual matters: the Inquisition, the *signatura* (which dealt with legal cases, some of which were also concerned with religious questions), new churches, rites, the *Index of Forbidden Books*, clergy in religious orders, diocesan clergy and prelates, printing, and how to interpret questions that emerged from the implementation of Trent's decrees (called the Congregation on the Council). Courts were also set up for matters of theology and conscience, appeals, and civil cases. Administratively, there were offices for documents (the chancery), Church offices and marriage dispensations (the datary), finances (the apostolic *camera*), and state matters. In 1622, the Congregation for the Propagation of the Faith was added to oversee the missions growing quickly beyond Europe.

Maybe the best way to summarize this top-down, administrative, and even monarchical concept of the Church came from the Jesuit Robert Bellarmine, who early in the seventeenth century described the Church in these sentences (from one of his books on *Controversies*). They demonstrate the fact that the papacy had to compete with other monarchies and bureaucracies of the age:

> The one true Church is the community of humans brought together by profession of the true faith and communion in the same sacraments, under the rule of

recognized pastors and especially of the sole vicar of
Christ on earth, the Roman Pontiff.... [The Church is
indeed a community of humans] as visible and palpable
as the community of the Roman people, or the king-
dom of France, or the republic of Venice.[3]

But the Church's organization did not operate
exclusively at the top during these centuries. Trent
empowered bishops to implement its reform decrees
and bring the Church back to life. The council had
mandated that bishops live in their dioceses, since
absenteeism had long been a problem and a very legitimate complaint by both Catholic and Protestant
reformers. Bishops had to meet in provincial councils
under their archbishops once every three years, and
each diocese's clergy had to meet under its bishop in an
annual synod. The frequency of these meetings varied
from place to place: Germany had only a few, but a fair
number met regularly in Spain and Italy.

The Church faced several challenges: to balance
local independence and culture with Roman centralization, to insure that Roman Catholic doctrines and
sacraments be the same wherever they were taught and
celebrated, and to balance papal authority with episcopal authority. To work toward achieving these balances
and meeting these challenges, Pope Sixtus V and his
successors made sure that bishops of each region came
to Rome on a regular schedule: once every three to ten
years, based on how far they were from Rome. These
ad limina ("to the threshold/doorway") visits, which
had begun in the Middle Ages, continue to this day.
The bishops had to send their decisions and the reports

of their synods to Rome's Congregation on the Council for approval, so they were not independent. Nevertheless, they were also trying to operate within their area's particular circumstances and not simply impose a cookie-cutter Catholicism that disregarded local devotions and customs.

At the local level, bishops were now more concerned with asserting orthodoxy and uniformity with respect to training priests, examining them before ordination, supervising them by visiting their parishes, and gathering their insights and concerns by meeting with them periodically. Their goal was to make the parish the center of life, and attempt to balance liveliness with uniformity and orthodoxy. Parishes began to keep better records, especially for baptisms and marriages. So, even though the emphasis was undoubtedly on how the Church was organized from the top-down, this does not mean the Church was not living well from the bottom-up.

The Early Modern Church: A Continued Focus on the Head

As will be seen in many chapters of this book, Church developments in the early modern period were heavily influenced by increased secular political participation that led to revolution and more democratic governmental structures. The Enlightenment also challenged faith, as did the secularism and materialism that accompanied the Industrial Revolution. This occurred first in England, then spread across Europe, and ultimately to the new United States, starting in New England and spreading across the fast-growing country.

To defend herself against these challenges, the Church increasingly stressed her hierarchy, especially at the uppermost level of the papacy, and emphasized her authority over doctrine and discipline. This approach frustrated some Catholics who were participating in their secular governments but could not do so in a similar way in their Church. What dominated ecclesiology and related discussions of how the Church should be organized and governed was a sense that the Church was different from other governments or institutions: it was self-sustaining, dealt with matters both of this world and beyond it, and did not have to be in dialogue with political changes.

We have just seen how Robert Bellarmine, the Jesuit theologian who was later named a cardinal, discussed the Church as an institution as powerful and as rooted in the world as France or Venice. His idea remained influential in the early modern period, as the Church continued to recover from the Reformations. She also found herself under assault as just another monarchy, like the Bourbons overthrown during the French Revolution in 1789, or England's George III who was deposed as head of the colonies during the American Revolution a decade earlier. But for Bellarmine and others, the Church wasn't just another government. During this period, the phrase "perfect society" was used frequently: the Church was a perfect society. This did not mean that it held no sinners among its millions of members around the world, but rather that it was a self-sustaining organization with its own hierarchy, system of government, rules of order, levels of administration, and allegiance of its members. Clearly, this notion of a perfect society, at least in this version of its description, was an institutional conception that could clash with civil institutions.

Some American Catholics (and Catholics in other countries, too, both then and now), for example, wanted not the "Roman Catholic Church in America," but an "American Church" more closely adapted to American governmental structures. Indeed, we must remember that during this period, for the first time in history, the Church became truly universal because it was only after Columbus that Christianity existed around the globe. Missionaries were spreading the universal Catholic faith using the catechism, missal, and other materials that appeared after Trent. At the same time they were also adapting Catholicism to the lived experiences of the very diverse local cultures that they served. The missionaries relied on the administrative Roman Church and the structures that came down from her head, to be sure, but at the same time they saw the faith enlivened by the piety bubbling up from below.

So the Church's centralization had its resisters. In particular, attempts at local independence threatened the Church's autonomy. As a result, yet another brick was cemented into the defensive posture and siege mentality that characterized the Church's approach to the world during this period, especially after Napoleon took two popes as prisoners. Therefore, officials at the Church's highest levels spent their time making sure the Church's administrative structures were in order while defending Catholicism's monarch, the pope, against those inside the Church who wanted the Church to adapt to the democratic developments taking place outside the Church. So the Church became even more a closed structure, at least at its top, while down below the Church was diversifying around the world.

Nevertheless, by the 1840s nearly every discussion of the Church's organization and government took place in institutional and administrative terms. The discussion was always about authority, but it was rarely even a discussion; it was more a statement of fact. A theologian named Giovanni Perrone, for example, stressed that the Church really meant the pope and his bishops gathered together as the Church's teachers. Her teaching authority, the *magisterium,* did not leave room for participation for speculative theologians or lay people. It was the job of pope and bishops to teach. It was the job of the people, the laity below the clergy, to learn. While lay people received the Church's teaching, they were not in any way to question that teaching or participate in its formulation, acceptance or rejection, or subsequent reformulation. As a result, the notion of the people of God as an essential part of the mystical body of Christ largely vanished from conversation. This idea of the Church as all the people of God would have to wait until the end of the nineteenth century, and especially until the coming of Vatican II in the middle of the twentieth, to once again enjoy acceptance, as it had done in the early and medieval centuries of the Church's development.

The Modern Church: The People of God

MAJOR CHANGES WERE AT HAND and the impetus to develop was coming from the Church's fingers and toes.
European missionaries were gradually turning their
parishes and dioceses over to indigenous catechists and
ministers. Popes Benedict XV, Pius XI, and Pius XII in
the beginning and middle of the twentieth century gave
great support to the missions. They wanted to see priests
of the same ethnicities, cultures, and races as of the
parishioners they served. Ordinations of indigenous men
to the priesthood rose sharply after 1915, and ordinations
to the episcopacy naturally followed: six Chinese priests
were ordained bishops by Pope Pius XI in Rome in
1926, then a Japanese bishop followed the next year,
with a Korean bishop in 1937, and then the first modern
African bishop in 1939. (There had been North African
bishops during the early centuries, but once Islam took
hold of North Africa in the seventh century, Christianity
largely disappeared. While North Africa remains mostly
Muslim today, large sections of sub-Saharan Africa are
Christian and specifically Catholic.) Bishops from India
and Indonesia soon followed.

The next important step in modern ecclesiology
and discussions of Church organization and governance
came in 1943 with Pope Pius XII's encyclical *Mystici
Corporis*. In this statement, Pius XII stressed the centrality of the pope as the representative of Christ, the
Church's ultimate head, and the pope as successor to
the chief apostle Peter, who is Christ's vicar on earth.
Pope Pius XII called the bishops "the nobler members

of the universal Church," but noted that they are subordinate to papal authority. In the same encyclical, Pius XII also used more expansive theological language to talk about the Church as the mystical body of Christ, therefore resurrecting an idea from early and medieval ecclesiology. A hierarchy is at work, but it is not a question of a hierarchy *or* the mystical body, but rather a hierarchy *and* the mystical body—two ideas that neither compete nor cancel each other out.

The road was now open to Vatican II and especially to the document *Lumen Gentium,* which gathered all of these ideas together and tried to strike that delicate balance that had existed in varying degrees up until the late twentieth century. *Lumen Gentium* spent time discussing the Church as the people of God and the mystical body of Christ while also acknowledging the bishops' leadership and their role as the apostles' successors. *Lumen Gentium* also acknowledged the primacy of the pope as both a member of the college of bishops and the head of that college. Here we have a conception of the Church that is multilayered and tries hard to balance centuries of various images, offices, notions, and experiences of how the Church should operate.

Of course, the Church is truly global and needs administrative structures, as would any organization with a billion members. In fact, the Vatican bureaucracy is comprised of many types of offices, the most important of which for the average Catholic are the congregations and councils headquartered in Rome. There are congregations for the doctrine of the faith, Eastern Churches, worship and sacraments, saints, bishops, priests and deacons, evangelization, religious orders, and education. The councils grew out of Vatican II's specific and new concerns. They operate more as advisory bodies rather than decision-making groups, which is what the congregations are. The councils deal directly with the laity, Christian unity, interreligious dialogue, the family, justice and peace, charity, care of migrants, pastoral care of health care workers, interpretation of canon law questions, culture (meaning the arts), and mass media.

Finally, we must acknowledge that questions remain. Pope John Paul II was a very centralizing pope, while at the same time he reached out to literally touch Catholics around the world as no pope in history has ever been able to do before, thanks to modern technology. As a result, some theologians supported his papal centralization, while others, bishops and cardinals among them, were concerned that he stressed the papacy too much at the expense of the local bishop, regional groups of bishops, national episcopal conferences, and the college of bishops as it exists theoretically worldwide (but never gathers as such outside a general council). Pope John Paul was very much concerned with having synods of bishops gather not only in Rome, but in central locations throughout the world. However, some theologians and bishops complain that these meetings are nothing more than rubber stamps of decisions that the pope has already made. They would like a more participatory assembly or at least a larger role played by the bishops and theologians on site in setting a synod's agenda.

Others complain that the idea of collegiality—of the bishops as equal members of the college of bishops, and therefore of the pope as just another member of the college since he is bishop of Rome—has been lost. (Of course, the pope is the only bishop who is at the same time a member and the head of the college of bishops, so his is a difficult dance in the best of circumstances.) Another issue is subsidiarity: some bishops would like local decisions to be made locally, or at least in the context of a national episcopal conference, with no recourse to Roman approval. Once more, the question is: what is the relationship between the local Church and the pope in Rome? Ironically, then, the Church today finds herself asking many of the same questions she asked in her first centuries, but now she has many more years of experience, mistakes, achievements, and wisdom from which to draw.

Chapter 2

THE LAITY

What has been the changing role of lay people?

The Early Church: Establishing an Identity

Since Vatican II, so much attention has been paid to lay people that we might think lay participation is something new. While the decades since the 1960s have indeed seen many changes in lay ministry and activities, lay people have long played a vital part in Church history. But that road to Vatican II was certainly not a continuous line of increasing recognition. Let's start at the beginning, then.

The first thing to notice about lay people from the historical evidence of the early Church is something that's not there: namely, a very firm type of distinction between "laity" and "clergy" as we understand those terms today. Only gradually, over time and growing out of the natural development of the Church, did particular people take on certain roles within the Church. It is very important to keep in mind that, although some of these developments were conditioned by historical events, it is also clear that there were the seeds of different "orders" within the Church community from the very beginning. No one made them up later in history. And no one thought that certain orders were better or higher than others—only that they were distinct, separate, and had different roles to play.

We can't find the word "laity" in the Old Testament or the New Testament—at least a "laity" as distinct from a "clergy." But we often find the important word *laos*, which at various places in the Bible indicates a people, a nation, Israel, and the new people of God. The word *laos* in the Bible denotes not only "ministers," but those they served; no clear distinction was yet made, although the Hebrew people did have a priestly class with specific liturgical functions, especially in the Temple.

The Old Testament contains the idea of a "new people of God" who believed in one divinity, which separated them from their polytheistic and pagan neighbors in the ancient Mesopotamian and Mediterranean worlds. This "new people of God" naturally became a "new people of Christ" in earliest Christianity. By the middle of the first century, we begin to find the word "laity" rarely, though it probably refers to this "new people of Christ" and not a particular class of lay people as opposed to a separate group of clergy. But as the second century proceeds, a division begins to appear between the *ordo* ("order") of people in leadership positions who had been ordained in some way and the *ordo* of people who were not, though some of these may have also been involved in ministry or even leadership of some type. Early Christians who were not ordained nevertheless acted as ministers of charity, teachers, and apologists—just as they do today. But only the ordained could celebrate the Eucharist and preside at the sacraments.

By the middle of the third century, some distinctions had been made among God's people who believed in Jesus Christ. There were ordained ministers: men who celebrated the sacraments and received the laying on of hands and sometimes an anointing. This *ordo* of the clergy was marked by their "ordination": these men were what we today call priests and the leaders among them were bishops. Each community had one bishop, so this system was called "monepisco-pacy." Both priests and bishops received an ordination from higher authorities: priests from bishops, and bishops from other bishops.

Lay people, meaning those who were not ordained, exercised ministry, too. Lay ministers were selected by the community, priests, and bishops. Everyone would pray over them, but the priests and bishops typically laid hands on them to confer a special blessing on the work they would do for their fellow Christians, such as the poor, the widows, and the orphans. They were not ordained. Some of these lay people chose to withdraw from the world and live a life of chastity and asceticism; these were the first "monks" and "nuns," to use later terms. Typically, they lived together in small communities, often in rural settings, and sometimes alone. Most of these first ascetics in the earliest "monastic" settings were also not ordained.

While some people might say that the clergy "withdrew" from the world because they did not concern themselves with worldly matters or did not marry and have families (although not all priests were celibate at this time) and lay people lived "in the world," this is a false distinction. The state of being a lay person and being a clergy member was increasingly not based on *where* people lived their Christian lives, but on *how*—what actions they performed and how the Church officially sanctioned those actions: with ordination or without ordination. In turn, certain actions were associated with the different states of life: priests led liturgies and lay people participated in them by praying, singing, walking in processions, receiving Communion, seeking penance, and taking part in other devotional and service actions. Each had their particular role.

Examples abound of lay people living their faith as actively as the ordained ministers. Many lay people kept the faith along with their clergy members during the Roman persecutions in the first four centuries of Christianity. They earned the crown of martyrdom with their priests and bishops—and sometimes without them, when some priests and bishops denied being Christians in order to save their lives. In North Africa and the East especially, lay people were involved in Church affairs as teachers, catechists, and theologians, taking part in the great debates concerning doctrine. The theologian and bishop Gregory Nazianzus reported that he heard lay people arguing about Christ's humanity and divinity in the markets of Constantinople in 379.

In fact, in the nineteenth century, when the British theologian John Henry Newman (1801–1890) wanted to demonstrate the important role the laity should play in Church matters in his own day, he turned back to early Church history. In these great theological debates of the fourth century he found an example of vibrant lay participation. Newman claimed that Church doctrine was sometimes kept whole and unstained more often by the laity than by their bishops, especially after the First General Council of Nicaea in 325. Nicaea had proclaimed Jesus' divinity against the heresy of Arius, who said Jesus was a kind of super-human, but not divine. Despite this statement, Arianism persisted for another fifty years and some bishops let it live.

Newman believed that faithful lay Christians kept the true faith during those years and should be consulted in his own day on what the content of that faith actually is. Arian bishops even opposed some of these Christians, while others literally walked away from bishops who taught doctrine about Jesus that was contrary to Nicaea's orthodox teaching. Clearly, then, the laity were not second-class citizens in the early Church.

The First Millennium Church: A Developing Role

AFTER THE ROMAN EMPIRE FIRST tolerated Christianity and then established it as the only official and legitimate religion (in the fourth century), a clearer line emerged between an unordained laity and an ordained clergy. Still, the idea of a lay *ordo* living in the world and a clerical *ordo* living apart from the world remained nothing more than a caricature without a strong basis in reality. Especially as Rome collapsed, priests and bishops became leaders in the provincial cities of the former Roman Empire. They offered service not only to the Church, but also to civil society by negotiating treaties, collecting taxes, overseeing public welfare, and maintaining roads and bridges.

The more powerful and wealthier laity, meanwhile, also served the Church by working as advisors to these clerical leaders as well as to the many lay rulers of local areas throughout Europe and the East. However, an unfortunate tendency began in this period as the two orders separated: to see the laity as a second or lower class of Christians, allegedly because they did not lead lives of poverty, chastity, and obedience. Not every priest or bishop did, either, and as we have seen, both orders had worldly duties that they often carried out faithfully and honorably. Still, the history books have painted this as a period where laity walked an inferior, lower, or secondary pilgrim journey in the faith. Because people thought that the clerical *ordo* was a "better," "higher," or even "purer" way to live the faith, the idea arose that to be a better Christian, one had to join the clergy. Since the clergy were becoming leaders of society, the path to political power sometimes ran through a church's aisles and schools, and not down a strictly lay road.

Some of these histories paint lay people as passive and even negative—certainly an unfair characterization. More recent studies have identified a very vibrant faith life for lay men and women struggling to keep the faith during these harsh centuries. Toward the end of the first millennium, evidence shows lay people gathering to share particular devotions (such as to a local saint) or service activities (like caring for their area's poor). In addition, the local priest was close to the laity of his village, since he often came from a local family and spoke their dialect, which included preaching in the vernacular during Mass. So, in the experience of the overwhelming majority of Christians in these centuries, the face of the Church for lay people was not a remote and rich cleric, but one of their own who lived and worked with them, sharing their poverty and lay sensibilities.

We should also distinguish between the relatively few lay aristocrats at the upper crust of society and the crowds of peasants below. From the fifth century through the Middle Ages, the monks, theologians, and bishops who wrote Church history did not refer to what we might call blue-collar Christians when speaking of "the laity." Instead, they meant the highest echelons of society: nobles and royalty. When bishops say that "the laity" should have no role in Church affairs, they did not mean that a parishioner should not complain about a sermon, but that a duke should not try to appoint his brother-in-law as an abbot or bishop, and thereby try to control the Church's power, money, and influence.

Of course, some of these richer laity were well-disposed to the Church and gave time, effort, and huge amounts of money to build churches, convents, monasteries, and centers of learning to spread the faith. Starting in the fourth century, Roman emperors in the eastern half of the Empire called for regional and ecumenical Church councils and paid the expenses of the traveling bishops, theologians, and advisers—some of whom were laymen. The Byzantine Empress Irene called, supervised, and even addressed an extremely consequential general council, Nicaea II, in 787, which solved the iconoclast controversy by deciding that Christians could venerate relics and icons. Charlemagne, who ruled most of central Europe in the late 700s and early 800s, was a great protector of the faith as a layman. His centers of learning trained priests and lay scholars—which promoted both partnership and tension between clergy and laity. He and his son, Louis the Pious, were seen as new Constantines who endowed the churches, protected the poor, promoted higher learning as well as basic catechesis, and tried to mediate disputes so that peace, justice, and the faith might spread.

At the same time, monasteries and convents were full of people who were essentially lay men and women, not "monks" and "nuns" in any clerical sense. Benedict's *Rule* from the sixth century stipulated that priests should not have special privileges, and that a monastic community should only ordain enough priests to satisfy the liturgical and sacramental needs of the rest of the community. Furthermore, these monasteries and convents enjoyed a measure of independence from a bishop's oversight and were often self-sustaining Christian communities of lay people. By the end of the first millennium, monasticism was nearly its own *ordo*. A split was developing, however, between a small group of ordained monks and a larger group of lay brothers, who were not as well-educated as the clerical monks, and who did the manual labor for them. Greater change appeared on the horizon, however: as the Middle Ages approached, the clergy-lay divide split wider, with lay people coming into their own much more than they had during the darker centuries of the first millennium.

The Medieval Church: A High Point for the Laity

THE CHURCH IN THE MIDDLE AGES witnessed a solidification of clerical and lay roles. When we visit museums, libraries, or cathedrals, the art and architecture may make us think that only literate monks and bishops dominated medieval Christianity. But side-by-side with them in the golden age of Christianity in the Middle Ages, a vibrant laity was involved in apostolic acts, confraternities, pilgrimages, religious festivals, and a wide range of other activities.

Before we get to these activities, we should consider the delineation between laity and clergy in the Middle Ages. As in the later centuries of the first millennium, Church leaders had a legitimate concern to restrict lay interference in the appointment of bishops and abbots. They had a positive goal—to keep the Church free from outside interference—and the "laity" concerned were the very few nobles at the highest, wealthiest, and most powerful levels of society. In 1296, for instance, Pope Boniface VIII in a papal bull (*Clericis laicos*) said harshly: "That laymen have been very hostile to the clergy, antiquity relates; and it is clearly proved by the experiences of the present time. For not content with what is their own, the laity strive for what is forbidden and loose the reins for things unlawful."[1] He was protesting an attempt by France's king to tax the clergy without papal approval. Clearly, "the laity" in *Clericis laicos* is not referring to the many Christians in the pews, but to the very few on thrones.

The Church's general councils, especially the four Lateran Councils held in the century from 1123 to 1215, issued many canons and disciplinary decrees concerning the clergy. These seem to be intended to separate them from the laity. The canons noted the qualifications for ordination, as well as restricted clergy from dressing as lay people and taking part in "worldly" activities (gambling, acting, and being involved in activities that included the shedding of blood such as fighting in the army). In seeking to regulate their conduct and dress, these rules helped bring about a very clear demarcation between clergy and laity. Unfortunately, this division led to the idea that one state of living was higher than the other. But it may have been that the Church's bishops were merely trying to be clear: this is what the clergy and the laity are and are not, what they should and should not do.

More positively, we can speak about lay religious activities. The medieval lay man and woman certainly did not live a sterile, Sunday-only faith. Christianity was a vibrant and daily exercise, since the Middle Ages lived and breathed the faith. The many saints' days, especially of local saints, were holidays, and church bells marked time in the towns. Medieval people wouldn't have used these terms, but they lived the spirit of Vatican II's 1965 document *Gaudium et Spes* by linking their daily work lives "in the world" with their faith. They prayed for good crops, gave offerings to local shrines, and celebrated the bigger feast days by staging, acting in, or attending morality plays, Passion plays, and plays on the lives of the saints. Many of these activities coincided with harvest festivals, liturgical seasons like Advent and Lent, and the major feasts of Christmas and Easter.

This period also saw an increase in the number of lay people recognized as saints, first in their communities, then by the local bishop, and finally through Rome's procedures for canonization. A fair number of medieval lay people were declared saints, making them models and heroes for everyone in the Church. As might be expected, lay brothers and sisters in monasteries and convents, along with royalty and nobles, won canonization. But so did lay soldiers, merchants, bankers, shopkeepers, artisans, male and female peasants, and "housewives." In the Middle Ages, the number of clerical saints dropped while the relative percentage of lay saints rose. The list of canonized saints included more women and more persons of humble origins. Nearly half of all royal saints were female, and women saints often gained notice for their roles as healers and miracle workers.

One of the largest movements in the Middle Ages was an upsurge in lay spirituality called the poor men's movements in which men, and sometimes women, decided to live a radical life of poverty and preaching. They reacted against the worldliness of the upper clergy—meaning the bishops in the larger cities, the cardinals, and the pope—by seeking in the Gospel a Christianity that was pure because it was poor. Although some of the movement's followers fell into heresy and preached without having a Church license to do so, the majority upheld orthodox teaching and wanted to identify with Christ as much as possible in their daily, lay lives.

Lay men and women also flocked to the kind of everyday spirituality represented by the *devotio moderna* of the late fourteenth century in northern Europe. They listened to preachers who encouraged them to look upon their lay state as workers, husbands and wives, mothers and fathers as their unique, holy vocations and not as a state of Christian life lower than the clergy's. Unfortunately, this attitude sometimes translated into too much criticism of the clergy. Some priests, bishops, and cardinals had a worldly and wealthy lifestyle, to be sure, but they were the minority. However, some of the more radical lay people began to taint all of the clergy, including the poor priests in their own villages and towns, with the unseemly actions of a few of the higher clergy. While this criticism was certainly justified in some situations, in the worst case it translated into anti-clericalism among some laity. Now it was the laity and not the Church leaders who were deepening the divide between laity and clergy. This situation would cause many problems in the next period of Church history.

The Reformation Church: Questions and Answers

HISTORY PROFESSORS USED TO USE an old line: bad priests caused the Protestant Reformation. While many clergy members, especially in the highest power positions, were immoral and worldly, this sentiment exaggerates the situation. In fact, recent scholarship illustrates that lay people and the priests who lived among them called for reform because of rising, not falling, expectations and standards.

Literacy was on the rise at this time. With the new printing press making pamphlets affordable, a kind of popular press—the tabloids of their day—hit the scene exactly when Protestants and Catholics were arguing about what kind of Church they saw as authentic. For those who couldn't read, inexpensive woodcuts in the pamphlets got the message across just as well. In addition, Martin Luther (1483–1546) published his criticisms, changes, and ideas on the Church in German; and Jean Calvin (1509–1564) did the same in French. People could read in their own languages and get involved in the conversations and debates without knowing Latin. Bibles were translated, too, so Christians could read them for themselves, especially the Gospels and St. Paul's key writings. A problem arose, however, because few people understood how to interpret Scripture, but they kept on trying. In this same vein, Protestants said almost anyone could preach, so lay people with very little learning began to spread a range of ideas.

These very active, not passive, lay people saw their faith as something to be lived and not just followed. A large majority of lay people, starting in the Middle Ages, criticized the clergy not because they wanted to get rid of priests or bishops, but because they felt some of them were not living the way they should. This sentiment sparked the criticisms offered by the humanist Erasmus that predated Luther's by a few years. He often had harsh words for bad priests, but was very encouraging toward lay people, whom he said should be fully Christian wherever God had placed them. Erasmus wanted weavers and plowmen to sing the psalms in their workshops and fields. Not only men, but women, too, should read the Gospels and St. Paul's letters. Ditch diggers,

Erasmus said, should know theology and the truths of the faith, which is their birthright as baptized Christians.

When positive (and sometimes justified) criticism of priests crossed into anti-clericalism, troubles began. Some lay people thought that all Christians were priests and that there should not be any division whatsoever between laity and clergy. Luther taught that ministry was an office or a function, but that it was not necessary to have a class of people, the clergy, set aside to exercise this office or function. Priesthood, for Luther, was not a state or a sacrament and priests should be appointed (not ordained) by the people (not the hierarchy), and not necessarily for their whole lives. They were ministers only when acting as ministers, not at other times. Luther taught that Baptism makes everyone a priest because all Christians share in the duties and powers of the priesthood of Christ, who is the one and only true priest that the Church needs. The only "indelible" mark is that of the baptized Christian; ordination does not change a person forever ("indelibly"). Anyone could celebrate the sacraments and preach, provided they had been properly selected and commissioned—although Luther restricted this function to men and excluded women from ministry.

These ideas gave rise to the phrase "the priesthood of all believers." Depending on your perspective, this concept either elevated the laity to the status of clergy, or reduced the clergy to the status of lay people. Both perspectives, of course, propagated the idea of a hierarchy of vocations. In fact, both Protestants and Catholics turned to lay and priestly formation, although from very different perspectives, in the years after the first generation of the Protestant Reformation in the first half of the sixteenth century. Protestants worked out the implications of the priesthood of all believers (laity and ministers). The idea of laity and lay vocation spread quickly and positively throughout the Protestant denominations. Many leading laymen were, in fact, former priests. Not all of them continued in ministry: they became theologians, lawyers, and merchants, and many worked in the book trade as artists, writers, translators, and printers.

Meanwhile, the Catholic Church at the Council of Trent reaffirmed priesthood as a sacrament with an indelible mark. It reasserted that priests could not marry and had to be celibate, and it said that the clergy was indeed a separate category apart from the laity. The Church also absolutely asserted that only an ordained priest could celebrate the sacraments and only ordained deacons and priests could preach. But right after Trent adjourned in 1563, and then throughout the next few centuries, bishops also spent a great amount of time, energy, effort, and money in improving catechesis among lay people. Church leaders trained teachers, many of whom were lay men and women, and organized them into the Confraternity of Christian Doctrine (CCD) of that era. Bishops also focused lay religious activities around confraternities and sodalities, which were groups of like-minded people who were drawn to a particular devotion (such as the Sacred Heart of Jesus or the Rosary) or saint (either of local interest, like St. Ambrose, or universal, like St. Joseph or Mary). Unlike what happened in the Middle Ages, however, during the Reformation these lay groups lost some of their independence and autonomy. The Church required them to be affiliated with a certain priest, parish, religious order, or some other ecclesiastical authority. Given the breakaway of Protestants and the swirling of ideas that were competing with Catholicism and confusing Catholics, the Church was naturally more cautious about these groups.

Finally, many lay people, both Protestants and Catholics, died for their faith in the conflicts and wars fought at least partly (and without doubt unfortunately) in the name of religion in these centuries. They were martyrs for Christianity, regardless of their Protestant or Catholic faith. Christians were killing Christians in these battles. The most famous on the Catholic side, Sir Thomas More, was a lay man who literally lost his head in 1535 when he stood up to King Henry VIII. Thomas said that a lay king, no matter how powerful, could not set himself up as an authority over the Church led by the highest cleric: the pope.

The Early Modern Church: New Challenges

THE EARLY MODERN PERIOD OFFERED new challenges for lay people: that of living a faith-filled life at all, especially in democratic societies that were sometimes hostile to religious loyalties. In these centuries, European Catholics were on occasion seen as superstitious, and therefore opposed to the rationalism and secularism of the Enlightenment. They were also accused of being ultimately faithful not to their countries, but to the pope. This allegiance competed with the national pride toward one's country that became stronger during this early modern period. Moreover, leaders of the French Revolution and similar, smaller outbreaks of violence throughout Europe saw the papacy as another monarchy to topple, the clergy as another privileged class to overthrow, and lay Catholics as disloyal aliens to these political and social goals. Clergy and laity were subject to suspicion and assault from enemies outside the Church, while sometimes competing with each other within the Church. Meanwhile, in the lands that were colonized after the Age of Discovery, new lay people entered the Church. This in turn raised novel questions: could slaves and indigenous people receive the Eucharist and fully share in the sacramental life of the Church? Could the men among them be ordained priests?

We can see two major developments for lay people in these circumstances: one mainly in Europe and the other in the new United States.

The first major development came from the spirituality promoted by Francis de Sales (1567–1622) and Jane Frances de Chantal (1572–1641). They both died just on the threshold of early modernity, but their ideas had a lasting impact throughout the period that followed their ministries. In a long friendship whose ideals are preserved in many letters, de Sales and de Chantal called everyone to live the Christian life fully, regardless of their lay or clerical state. In fact, lay people followed these ideas a bit more enthusiastically and in greater numbers than the clergy. Perhaps this was because the laity was looking for an identity in these difficult times after the Protestant Reformation and the Council of Trent. Those events were followed by the Scientific Revolution and Enlightenment, which brought new challenges to faith.

De Sales and de Chantal called lay men and women to love God as much as they could within one's circumstances—that is, to live a devout life. De Sales described this love as having two arms: one in prayer and one in service. Together, they offered a very positive notion of the material world, turning back any remaining notion of *contemptus mundi* from the first millennium and Middle Ages while anticipating the openness of Vatican II in the 1960s. They gave very practical advice on daily work, marriage, and family life. They realized that, given the pressures of these obligations, prayer must often be short. And that was fine: prayer was good and pleasing to God, even if it had to be cut short because of the need to give charitable service to family and friends. The interactions between human beings in the everyday details and ordinary nature of daily life gave opportunities for lay men and women to be Christ, in humble service and interdependence, for each other. One didn't have to perform monastic acts of self-mortification to achieve this goal of purification: doing what no one else wanted to do— like washing the dishes or scrubbing the laundry or milking the cow at dawn—was a path to God.

The second major development occurred in the United States and began just about the time the colonists officially won their independence from the British Empire. Catholics were a very small minority at the end of the eighteenth century. The Bill of Rights gave them the freedom of religion they had not enjoyed when the American colonies were British and therefore officially part of the Church of England. Lay Catholics exercised their newfound freedoms, especially from the late 1700s to the eve of the American Civil War, by practicing a Catholicism informed and fueled by the fierce independence that made the colonies break away from Great Britain. Trouble came because American Catholics did not share the history and sensibilities of many European Catholics, especially when it came to deferring to the jurisdiction of the papacy and the clergy. American Catholics, after all, were democratic Americans who had just overthrown a king's authority. They were "the people" of the Church as they were "the people" of the United States.

This impulse manifested itself in trusteeism, by which lay Catholics said that they owned and controlled churches, schools, and even the priests assigned to them. This brought up issues of governance and authority: Who owned a parish? Who could buy and sell its property? Who could make decisions about a parish, its pastor, or its programs? How was the parish related to its pastor and bishop? What kind of authority did the pastor and bishop have with respect to the parish? This was worked out through a parish's board of trustees, composed largely or even exclusively of lay people, who said they owned the parish, its properties, and its finances. Therefore, it was up to these lay people and not the pastor or bishop to pay the bills, order and oversee new building projects or programs, and hire and fire employees from the parish secretary to its priests and pastor—some said bishop, too. They were happy to leave the sacraments to the priests, but that should be the end of the clergy's mandate.

Obviously, priests, pastors, and bishops did not agree with this arrangement. Unfortunately, the resulting battles turned ugly as clergy and laity fought by using the typical, tired, and adversarial us-versus-them language of clericalism, anti-clericalism, and the hierarchy of vocations. This resulted in a series of religious and legal conflicts. Parishes and dioceses were split apart in cities with sizable and wealthy Catholic populations: New York City, Buffalo, Boston, Philadelphia, Baltimore, Norfolk, Charleston, and New Orleans. The American bishops fought back in 1829 with a firm statement that they were in charge of parishes, had financial control of their dioceses and its properties, and held the exclusive right to hire and fire priests and pastors. Like bishops in other countries, American bishops saw this attempt to apply democracy or republicanism to the Church as a Protestant or congregationalist model that was not in keeping with Roman Catholic teaching and tradition. It was an uprising that had to be put down, which the bishops successfully did in the 1830s–1850s. They used Church and civil law to help them regain financial control of their parishes and dioceses.

The Modern Church: A Renewed Vision

IT WOULD BE INCORRECT TO SAY THAT the modern period is the most lay-driven or lay-involved in history, since we have seen that lay men and women have always played an important part in the Church's life. But it is still true that from the middle of the nineteenth century, and especially since Vatican II (1962–1965), lay people have been involved more prominently, more influentially, and in more leadership positions than perhaps at any other time in Church history. The old line that the laity's job was only to "pray, pay, and obey" has certainly not been true in the modern Church.

The person who really gave the laity a kind of justifying theology of their own was in fact a member of the clergy: the British priest and later Cardinal John Henry Newman. As we have already seen, it was Newman the Church historian who saw in the fourth century a model for lay orthodoxy. He identified the fact that many lay people kept the true faith in Jesus' humanity and divinity even as some bishops after the Council of Nicaea maintained the Arian heresy that Jesus was not quite God. Writing in the second half of the nineteenth century, Newman called for the laity to be well-educated, to be leaders in their parishes and the wider Church, and even to be consulted on matters of doctrine. Because he stressed that the entire mystical body of Christ—the Church—holds the faith firmly and truly, Newman said that when Church authorities were defining doctrine, they should listen to the lay people to hear what people already believed and have always believed. (In fact, Pope Pius IX had made just such an inquiry before defining the dogma of the Immaculate Conception in 1854.) A British bishop responded to Newman's championing such an essential role for the laity by dismissively asking, "Who are the laity?" Newman famously replied: "The Church would look foolish without them."

Change was certainly in the air during this period. The current *Code of Canon Law* was revised in 1983 and contains more and greater treatment of the laity than the previous 1917 edition. More attention, and we might even say respect, is paid to lay people's equality as believers as well as to their rights, particular mission and vocation, and their access to theological formation on basic and advanced levels. Indeed, canon 229 paragraphs 1 and 2 are worth quoting:

> Lay persons are bound by the obligation and possess the right to acquire knowledge of Christian doctrine appropriate to the capacity and condition of each in order for them to be able to live according to this doctrine, announce it themselves, defend it if necessary, and take their part in exercising the apostolate.
>
> They also possess the right to acquire that fuller knowledge of the sacred sciences which are taught in ecclesiastical universities and faculties or in institutes of religious sciences, by attending classes there and pursuing academic degrees.

While another canon (212, paragraph 1) notes that the laity are obligated to demonstrate obedience to their pastors, paragraph 2 of that same canon says lay people are free to tell their pastors of their needs and desires. Paragraph 3 says that lay people "have the right and even at times the duty" to give their opinions, based on their experience and knowledge, about matters affecting the Church.

Vatican II devoted a document to the laity, titled *Apostolicam Actuositatem,* although the laity appear in many of the fifteen other documents that the council promulgated. *Lumen Gentium,* for instance, gave perhaps the clearest and most refreshing sentence on the matter: "The apostolate of the laity is a sharing in the Church's mission of salvation, and everyone is commissioned to this apostolate by the Lord himself through Baptism and Confirmation" (no. 33). This same document sought a greater mutual respect between clergy and laity, asking pastors to allow lay people to exercise their proper ministries in the parish, while stressing that the laity bore a special duty to share Christianity where they worked, particularly in secular settings.

It was exciting to hear that lay people had vocations. Simply using that word "vocation," which too often had been applied exclusively to a priest or nun, raised the prestige and standing of the lay person. Laity learned that they had a special and equal vocation. Some of the bishops gathered in Rome for the council identified clericalism as an enemy of the Church, which reminds us that both clericalism and anti-clericalism harm the clergy and laity of the Church in any age.

Apostolicam Actuositatem recognized that, in the modern age, the lay person's role had expanded and was growing daily more critical, not only to the Church, but also to the world. The role of lay women was seen as something that had to grow, become more vital, and move closer to the center of discussions, influence, and leadership. A new Vatican department was devoted to the laity and is today called the Pontifical Council for Laity. In addition, other councils treat lay issues directly: the Pontifical Council for the Family and the Congregation for Catholic Education. Indeed, another Vatican II document (*Gravissimum Educationis*) joined *Apostolicam Actuositatem* in stressing that the laity should be well-educated in the faith and that they should play a key educational role as teachers, catechists, and parents. Significantly, the document on the liturgy (*Sacrosanctum Concilium*) called for the laity's active participation in liturgy. The ecumenical document (*Unitatis Redintegratio*) identified the lay tasks in reaching out to people of other faiths, and the document on bishops (*Christus Dominus*) encouraged them to promote and support the lay vocation and apostolate.

Not only have lay Catholics transformed the faith, they have also moved into leadership roles in their countries, too. In the United States, for instance, Catholics moved away from the attacks upon them as immigrants. Once known and feared as the "Catholic hordes"—immigrants from the middle of the nineteenth to the beginning of the twentieth centuries— lay people have left the "Catholic ghetto" to which they had been consigned and are now major players in business, education, economics, and politics. Catholics sit on the United States Supreme Court, have occupied the Oval Office, fill boardrooms and judicial benches, teach at every educational level, and are clearly in the mainstream of American culture and power.

In their parishes, lay men and women serve as Eucharistic ministers, altar servers, lectors, and leaders for retreats, Bible study, sacramental preparation, and faith formation programs. What lay Catholics do with their power in both Church and civil arenas on the local and national levels will be part of the next, unwritten chapter of Church history.

Chapter 3

THE PAPACY

How did the papacy develop?

The Early Church: Humble Beginnings

WHEN PEOPLE (CATHOLIC OR NOT) think of "the papacy," they usually think immediately of the Vatican with its bureaucracy and ornate buildings. This does not mean, however, that the papacy's physical form indicates that it is a human institution. The papacy grew as it did in response to human events, true, but it was from the beginning established by Jesus in Peter.

The papacy began with a flawed fisherman whom the Romans executed as a criminal. Tradition says that Peter was the longest serving pope, at about thirty-five years, but this is not certain. The evidence shows that during the first few centuries of the Church, the popes were local leaders of a small, but growing, church in Rome, who did not immediately command the kind of universal authority that characterizes the papacy in later periods.

Before Peter and each of his successors was "the pope," he was "the bishop of Rome," but even this central office took time to develop. While we have a list of men identified as bishop of Rome for the first two centuries of the Church's life, the evidence suggests that Rome was served by several leaders who collectively led the local faith community, with perhaps one exercising a first-among-equals role. This was probably the case with Clement (91–101) at the end of the first century, who sent and received letters to Christians in other cities in the name of the Roman Christians. Anicetus (155–166) welcomed Polycarp of Smyrna on his visit to Rome. Soter (166–174) corresponded with the Corinthians. Eleutherius (174–189) interacted with

Irenaeus of Lyons. So the first popes, most of whom died as martyrs, seemed to be acting in the name of the Roman community without holding the kind of centralized and predominant authority we associate with medieval and modern popes.

Over time, and perhaps in reaction to a streak of local independence from other bishops in the early Christian communities along the Mediterranean Sea, some bishops of Rome began to emphasize the importance of Roman authority because Peter died in Rome. Peter's role as first among the apostles then settled on the shoulders of his successors, who were gradually seen to hold a special authority, such as to intervene in disputed questions or to confirm actions taken outside of Rome. Callistus I (217–222) was the first bishop of Rome to invoke Petrine authority explicitly, and Stephen I (254–257) used the phrase *cathedra Petri* (seat or chair of Peter) to describe Rome. When bishops who had gathered at Antioch in 341 did not inform Julius I (337–352) of their deliberations and actions, he grew angry and wrote to them: "Do you not realize that it has been the custom for word to be sent to us first, that in this way just decisions may be arrived at from this place?"[1] Two years later, in 343, a local council at Sardica recognized Julius' authority and right of appeal.

The papacy also developed because of geopolitics and even devotions. In 330, the Emperor Constantine moved to Constantinople; although a co-emperor remained in the West, the city of Rome began a slow decline. Into this power vacuum stepped the bishops of

Rome, who provided food, shelter, and a system of aid to the poor through city parishes and suburban centers. The attention paid to the martyrs, chief among them Peter, led many to commemorate graves with shrines, particularly in the catacombs. Peter's grave had been venerated on the Vatican Hill in the late second century, and Constantine ordered a basilica built there in the fourth century.

Important developments came under two successive bishops of Rome, Damasus I (366–384) and Siricius (384–399), who turned their reigns outward to exercise a wider authority beyond Rome. Damasus heard the appeals of bishops and took on the role of arbiter of disagreements and decisions. In 383, Damasus commissioned Jerome to translate the Bible into Latin. This new text served as a unifying force for Christians everywhere and helped to establish the bishop of Rome as a key authority on biblical interpretation and canonicity. Concerned that the bishop of Constantinople would try to nudge close to Roman authority because an emperor lived in Constantinople as well as Rome, Damasus noted that Rome's primacy came from Christ, through Peter. He was the first pope to use the word "apostolic" with reference to Rome. Later popes would often use this word when they wanted to emphasize that their authority found its source in Peter and therefore in Christ who had commissioned him.

Siricius intervened more directly in the affairs of other churches. He dealt with bishops in Gaul and Spain as if they were his inferiors and not his equals. He often sent instructions and opinions instead of waiting for appeals to his judgment. Under him, the papacy also borrowed from the nearby secular government by adopting the tone and style of the Roman imperial chancery to issue decisions, decrees, and prohibitions. By the time of Innocent I (401–417), the bishop of Rome was declaring that nothing done by the clergy, no matter how far away they were from Rome, could be considered settled definitively until the pope gave his approval.

Leo I (440–461) exemplifies this moment in the papacy's development. He was the first pope to apply to himself the ancient Roman title of a chief priest: *pontifex maximus.* Leo stepped up, more than any other pope, to become the leader of Rome because civil authority was weak: he negotiated with the Huns and Vandals so they would spare the city. He also put the bishop of Rome first among the bishops by establishing his primacy and leadership in setting doctrine. He approved the documents of the Council of Chalcedon in 451, for example, and struck out certain canons with which he disagreed. Building on the work of other popes, Leo emphasized in his sermons that the bishop of Rome exercised the princely authority of Peter. He said that Peter continued to lead the Church through the bishop of Rome, who was quickly becoming more "papal."

The First Millennium: Highs and Lows

IF LEO I FINISHED BUILDING THE FOUNDATION of the papacy, two popes who followed him constituted the first few floors.

Gelasius I (492–496) needed to make clear that Church leaders, especially the bishops of Rome, were independent of the political structures around them. Although the Roman Empire in the West had begun to collapse, it still showed signs of life. The popes emphasized that the Church was not a department of the empire, but an institution of even greater authority. In an important letter to the Roman emperor in the East, Anastasius, Gelasius said that two swords came from God: one temporal and one spiritual. Christ had given both of these to Peter, and therefore to the pope. The pope, in turn, could delegate the temporal sword to the civil authorities, who ultimately ranked below the pope. Gelasius stood on an important precedent established a century earlier when Ambrose, the bishop of Milan, excommunicated the Western emperor Theodosius for his role in a massacre. When the time came for Gelasius to reiterate this relationship to Anastasius, he reminded him that popes must answer for kings in heaven, so the spiritual sword must be higher than the temporal sword. Hereafter, popes addressed emperors as sons.

Lest it seem that popes in this second important era of Church history were only involved in political disputes, consider a great pastoral pope, Gregory I (590–604). He had been a civil official in Rome until he converted to Christianity and resigned his post to study Scripture and pray. His skills soon caught the eye of the Roman clergy, however, and they understood that his combination of personal holiness and professional diplomacy could serve the Church. Gregory fought his selection as bishop of Rome, seeing himself as unworthy to walk in Peter's footsteps, but he accepted it as God's will. Using an important phrase for the papacy, Gregory called himself "servant of the servants of God"—and saw himself primarily as chief shepherd, not as a ruler.

Gregory's career neatly sums up where the papacy stood during this moment. He had to be an administrator: he was the single largest landowner in Italy, and he led the territories later formally called the "papal states." But he was primarily a religious leader at a time when Christianity was still a mission religion. Gregory saw the papacy as the spearhead for spreading Christianity to those who did not know the faith (pagans) or to those who understood and taught it incorrectly (heretics) in north Italy, in central Europe, and as far away as the British Isles. He wrote a long rule or manual for priests along with scriptural commentaries and sermons that exhorted Christians to live a moral life.

Despite the papacy's achievements, during this same period popes and the rest of the Western, Latin bishops grew increasingly estranged from their brothers in the East. A difference in languages contributed to the split—Greek was spoken in the East and Latin in the West. Another reason concerned the pope's role with respect to four other very important cities in early Christianity: Antioch, Alexandria, Jerusalem, and Constantinople. Along with Rome, bishops called "patriarchs" governed the Church in these cities. Bishops in the East were largely willing to accept Rome's primacy because of Peter's presence in Rome, but they rejected the idea that this primacy equaled supremacy. They did not believe that any one see or diocese could unilaterally interfere with another. Instead, they thought that the ultimate authority in the Church was an ecumenical council, and the government of the Church existed among the five patriarchs together. Eastern bishops therefore rejected what they saw as too much papal action. Leo I rejected canon 28 of the Council of Chalcedon (451), which placed the bishop of Constantinople at the same rank as the Roman bishop, although holding a place second in line after Rome. Eastern bishops saw his rejection as a unilateral and improper act since they held that no bishop could simply refuse to follow what an ecumenical council had declared collectively.

Another issue concerned the Latin word *filioque:* this word meant that the Holy Spirit proceeds from God the Father "and the Son." The word *filioque* was alternately accepted and refuted in the West—Leo III (795–816) even put the Creed without this word in his church in Rome—but by about 1000, *filioque* was standard in the West. The issue between the popes and the Eastern bishops was not so much the theological doctrine as the way it was promulgated. The word *filioque* did not appear in the Creed of the Council of Constantinople (381), but it was later added in Latin translations in the West and taken as an article of Christian faith, most notably in seventh-century Spain. Because *filioque* was added outside the context of an ecumenical council, the East saw the addition as an abuse of Western (especially papal) authority over what should be shared governance.

Other differences emerged, too: whether to use leavened or unleavened bread for the Eucharist, whether clergy could marry, and what rules to adopt for fasting and liturgy. These differences culminated in the dark moment in 1054 when East and West excommunicated the other, but the trouble had been brewing for nearly the entire first millennium of Church history.

Another factor led to the split between the papally led West and the East: Islam. When the prophet Mohammed (ca. 570–632) died, Islam spread rapidly from what is today the Middle East (Mecca and Medina are in modern-day Saudi Arabia) across North Africa, up the Iberian Peninsula (modern Spain and Portugal), across the Pyrenees and into southern France. There, in 732, Charlemagne's grandfather, Charles Martel, defeated the Muslims at a battle near the cities of Poitiers and Tours, causing the Muslims to retreat over the mountains and settle firmly in Iberia for most of the next 700 years. As a result of this expansion during the first millennium, western Christianity was cut off from her eastern half.

What did this Islamic expansion mean for the papacy? One famous historian, Henri Pirenne (1862–1935), wrote that without Mohammad, there would have been no Charlemagne. The bishops of Rome could no longer look east to Constantinople for help or south to North Africa, where so many important theologians (such as Augustine) had worked. So popes had to look north for protection and expansion. This relationship was sealed spectacularly on Christmas day in 800 when the pope, in his own chapel in Rome, crowned Charlemagne emperor.

This reliance upon the Holy Roman Emperor brought its own troubles. Popes now had to struggle to emphasize their independence and ultimate authority, but in this period they often failed. Some of the papacy's darkest days occurred in the centuries from about 850 to 1050. Most popes had short reigns and some even met with violent deaths. But these bad times did not last: the stage was being set for the emergence of a strong papacy, even a papal monarchy, in the Middle Ages.

The Middle Ages: Centralizing the Power

The papacy's goal in the Middle Ages was to pull itself out of the close and sometimes-troubling relationship it had with royal authority. But it ended by setting itself up as a rival monarchy with its own imagery, curia, law, and even pomp. The giant who stands out among medieval popes is Gregory VII (1073–1085), although the popes who came just before and after him were all "Gregorian," because they aimed to make the Church free and independent of royal interference. The papacy led the efforts to name and regulate bishops and priests. To achieve this goal, the popes constructed the very idea and structure of the papacy on a scale greater than anything seen before in Church history. In fact, the very word for papacy, *papatus,* essentially appears for the first time in the late eleventh century.

The Gregorian popes built on earlier precedents to make their claims. They repeatedly referred to their apostolic authority and made sure the people to whom they sent letters knew that when you spoke to the pope, you spoke to Peter—and therefore Christ. Medieval popes took away from emperors the title of vicar of Christ and began regularly calling themselves both *vicarius Christi* and *vicarius Petri,* although Gelasius I may have used "vicar of Christ" or been addressed with this title. They appointed legates who were allowed to wear papal insignia and who bore the title "vicar of the pope." These legates spoke in the pope's name, traveling throughout Europe to deliver his judgments on kings and bishops alike. All the while they worked to ensure that a Christian's first loyalty was to the Church, not to the local lord.

One of the most important developments in this period occurred in the College of Cardinals, which popes used to solidify their own authority and spread the power of the papacy. Although cardinals had existed in some form for over 500 years, the medieval popes made the college more of an institution with certain rights and privileges—something like the ancient Roman Senate, a medieval royal curia, or today's presidential cabinet. Only the pope could name cardinals, and he increasingly appointed them from a broader geographic area throughout Europe. In the twelfth century alone, the popes named 300 new cardinals, although there were usually only a few dozen at any one time. They became the pope's inner circle in Rome and his voice, as legates, across Europe. As the papacy developed financial, legal, liturgical, and secretarial departments, the popes put cardinals in charge as their most trusted advisors, which made the college a training ground for future popes.

The cardinals' most important role was to elect the pope. Papal elections had to be free for two major reasons: to make sure the papacy was not controlled by a political power and to offer the best example of free elections to the rest of Christianity. Too many times in the prior two centuries, warring Roman families had chosen the popes. During the Middle Ages the process of the conclave developed. In 1059, Pope Nicholas II gave the cardinals the lead role in papal elections. A general council, Lateran III, in 1179, said that elections did not have to be unanimous to be valid: a two-thirds majority would suffice for a candidate's election. Another council, Lyons II, in 1274, gave the Church the conclave, which locked the cardinals away until they chose a pope. Not only was this measure intended as an attempt to cut off outside interference; it was also intended to speed the election along, as the Church had recently gone through nearly three years without a pope because the cardinals could not settle on one man.

The Middle Ages also witnessed two of the most difficult chapters in papal history: the Avignon papacy (1305–1378) and the Great Western Schism (1378–1417). Early in the fourteenth century, the popes moved to southern France for some very good reasons: it was safer than central Italy, where civil wars raged and emperors invaded. While the popes lived in Avignon, the French monarchy came increasingly to exercise too much pressure. Things in Avignon were not all bad, for some reform-minded popes ruled. But problems arose:

the papacy and the College of Cardinals became centralized, distant from the people, legalistic, wealthy, greedy, ambitious, luxurious, and overly French (with 85 percent of the cardinals named during this time being French). The Italian humanist Petrarch referred to the papal curia as the whore of Babylon and these decades as the Babylonian captivity of the papacy.

Hope flickered when Gregory XI moved the papacy back to Rome in 1377, but upon his death, the cardinals split in their conclave because the French wanted to return to Avignon. A tumultuous election in 1378 picked an Italian. Within a few months, however, the French cardinals said the election was invalid because the cardinals had fearfully caved in to the pressure of a Roman mob outside the conclave demanding an Italian pope. A few months later, these cardinals held a second election, picked a Frenchman, and eventually returned to Avignon. Each pope excommunicated the other pope and his College of Cardinals. Popes followed popes in both the Roman and Avignon lines for thirty years until a Church council at Pisa in 1409 tried to settle the matter. Pisa chose a new pope, but the Avignon and Roman popes refused to step down and recognize the new man. So now three popes and their three colleges of cardinals claimed supremacy until 1417. Then, the General Council of Constance finally got rid of the three rival popes and selected a unifying pope who received the allegiance of all of Christianity, ending almost forty years of schism.

The Avignon papacy and the Great Western Schism severely weakened the papacy's prestige. But even earlier, some writers had offered critiques of the papacy as a monarchy. In 1145, a student of Bernard of Clairvaux was selected to be Pope Eugene III. The pope wrote to his former teacher for advice and Bernard cautioned him that, as pope, he should be a servant, not a lord. "It is hardly fitting for you to be found relaxing in luxury or wallowing in pomp," Bernard wrote to the pope. "Does the throne flatter you? It is a watchtower. From it you oversee everything, exercising not dominion, but ministry."[2] Despite some good medieval popes, too many had become power brokers and caused trouble for the Church. Some of the developments of the medieval papal monarchy represented triumphs and achievements for the papacy, but others sowed the seeds of dissent and revolt that would occur during the Reformation.

The Reformations: Challenge and Response

This period of the papacy's history is sometimes referred to derisively as the Renaissance papacy, conjuring images of Borgias and Medicis fighting to put their sons on the papal throne, while the popes themselves had mistresses, children, and grandchildren, some of whom they named cardinals as teenagers. Unfortunately, some popes did indeed do such things—and worse, with Julius II (1503–1513) literally leading armies into battle. Acting as artistic patrons, popes in this period lavishly adorned churches and buildings by paying huge sums to the best craftsmen, artisans, sculptors, glaziers, and painters that money could buy—among them Michelangelo and Leonardo da Vinci.

These popes certainly had their critics. The most famous pundit, Erasmus, wrote a wicked satire called *The Praise of Folly* in which he said:

> ...[P]omp and pleasure are personally taken care of by the popes. They believe themselves to be readily acceptable by Christ with a mystical and almost theatrical finery.... [T]hey believe themselves to be justly called defenders of Christ, bragging that they have routed the enemies of the Church—as if the Church had any greater enemies than these charlatan popes who encourage the disregard of Christ, who depict Him as mercenary, who corrupt His teachings by forced interpretations, and who scandalize Him by their infamous lives.[3]

Certainly this era featured stereotypically corrupt and greedy "Renaissance popes" disconnected from the life of the average Christian and disdainful of Protestant criticisms. But during this age several popes tried to understand the valid points the reformers made in their critiques of Catholicism. Some of these popes tried to fix the problems that had caused huge sections of Christianity to break away from Rome.

Reading Church history, one might think that some popes just "didn't get it." Leo X (1513–1521) infamously dismissed Luther's posting of the *Ninety-Five Theses* in October 1517, and the theological debate it began, as just a quarrel among some German monks. But just a few years later, Hadrian VI (1522–1523), who had been influenced by Erasmus, told his legate to Luther's followers to make it clear he understood that many of the Church's problems started right at the top, with the papacy.

Once it was certain that Luther and the different reformers following him could not be reconciled with the Catholic Church, popes took different approaches to the situation. For example, many historians have pointed out the stark contrast between two popes named Paul. Pope Paul III (1534–1549) knew that some of the Protestant and Catholic criticisms of the Church and the papacy were justified. He brought to Rome reformers who did not work in the papal curia and had them write a long memorandum that spoke frankly and even harshly of how the papacy had become a corrupt bureaucracy. Paul III was also forward-looking: he supported new religious orders, such as the Jesuits, and turned the Church's attention to the missions in the Americas and Asia in the age of exploration. On the other hand, another pope named Paul, this one Paul IV (1555–1559), took the opposite tack: he steadfastly opposed the idea that the Church was flawed, supported institutions like the Inquisition and the *Index of Forbidden Books*, and adopted a generally repressive and defensive stance. He wanted to restore the kind of papal monarchy that reached back to Gregory VII's goals in the late eleventh century and the kind of authority Innocent III (1198–1216) had enjoyed. After the Council of Trent concluded in 1563, popes set up a more centralized Roman administration, with themselves as head and center of Catholicism.

Naturally, all of the popes after Luther defended the very existence, authority, and legitimacy of the papacy versus various Protestant claims that the papacy was an invention, an innovation, or an aberration that did not derive from Jesus. Perhaps the loudest and most instructive voice defending the papacy was that of Robert Bellarmine (1542–1621), a Jesuit who wrote a long treatise defending papal authority. At one point in the treatise, Bellarmine wrote a dialogue between the pope and the people. In it he stressed that papal authority held sway not only over the Christian congregations, but over any king who believed a king and not a pope had supreme authority on earth. "I am the shepherd appointed by Christ, who is the Lord of all the flock," the pope instructs the people. "You, the people, are the little sheep; your kings are the rams. As long as your kings continue to be rams, I permit them to rule and lead you. But if they turn into wolves, will it be right that I permit the sheep of my Lord to be led by wolves?"[4]

Not only did theology defend the papacy in this period, but architecture and liturgy did so, too. Popes supported the arts not only to be great patrons, but also to make the point that Rome was the center of Christianity. They set out to adorn the city where Peter died and, in so doing, to emphasize their authority as Peter's successor. The popes recreated the earliest Roman liturgies and provided funds for St. Peter's Basilica to stress this connection with Christianity's roots in Rome. They also extended their authority by appointing bishops who backed this centralized vision of the papacy. In addition, they sent their delegates to deal with other monarchs in Europe as equals or even inferiors. But this achieved only mixed results.

Many obstacles made it increasingly hard for the popes to maintain this notion of papal monarchy and supremacy. The Protestant Reformation had splintered Christianity from one Roman Catholicism into several Christian denominations, a situation that by its very nature tended to devalue the papacy as the one, only, and ultimate authority in Christian Europe. The known world itself had grown larger after Columbus. The papacy reacted in many ways. It strove to be relevant in a rapidly changing world in which secularism, rationalism, the Enlightenment, revolutions against monarchy, and Christian diversity challenged papal authority. The popes struggled to simply to keep up.

The Early Modern Church: Assaults from Many Sides

IN THE YEARS AROUND 1650–1850, all monarchies found themselves challenged, not just the papal monarchy that had developed during the Middle Ages and around the Council of Trent. Throughout the world, people began to call for greater participation in their government. They claimed that ultimate political power and authority rested in their hands, not in those of the government. This applied especially to divine-right monarchies, which claimed they held power because God had selected their families to reign. This period saw the American Revolution against King George III in England, the French Revolution against King Louis XVI and Marie Antoinette in France, and a series of such widespread revolts throughout Europe that historians refer to 1848 as "the year of revolutions."

The Scientific Revolution, the Enlightenment, and the Industrial Revolution brought great changes in Western society. Thinkers began to push religion aside and place man, not God, at the center of society. In a corresponding way, the papacy and the Church began to be devalued in certain circles as the new thinking undermined both the idea of faith and the notion of a universal religious authority. Monarchs and believers faced great challenges in that difficult time.

On top of these developments that rocked the papacy came another, which reached back to Church history. Since the early Middle Ages, the leaders of individual countries had to varying degrees claimed that they, and not the pope, wielded ultimate authority on Church matters in their kingdoms. They usually left matters of doctrine to the papacy, but on questions of Church governance, monarchs wanted to name their own bishops and make Christianity a department of the state. In this way, they asserted their own monarchical authority not only against the people calling for greater political participation, but against the papacy as a rival monarchy.

How did early modern monarchs try to overtake papal authority? One good example occurred in France. For centuries, a movement known loosely as "Gallicanism" held that the Church in France—or Gaul, to use the ancient Roman name—was in essence a church that was administratively separated from Rome while holding to the same dogmas. In 1682, reaching back to earlier precedents from the Middle Ages, the Gallican Articles were proclaimed. They said that the king, not the pope, held jurisdiction over the Church in France, that doctrine remained in the hands of the pope and the bishops, that a council of the Church was infallible, and that the Church in France was to be run as a state bureaucracy. A similar version, called Josephinism after the Emperor Joseph II who ruled central Europe in the late 1700s, called for the emperor to nominate bishops instead of the pope. All papal documents required the emperor's approval before they could be sent to the Church in Austria. The English kings William the Conqueror and Henry II had claimed precisely the same privileges in the late eleventh and twelfth centuries. The Austrian government cut off religious orders from their Roman superiors, and dissolved about a third of the religious houses.

The low point came in the late 1790s and early 1800s. Napoleon invaded Rome and took away parts of the papal states. He pushed Pope Pius VI (1775–1799) out of Rome and took him as a prisoner; the pope died in exile while in Napoleon's custody. The new pope, Pius VII (1800–1823), negotiated a return to Rome. But after Pius VII excommunicated the enemies who threatened him, Napoleon treated him just as he had treated the prior pope. He arrested Pius VII and kept him as a prisoner for five years. When Napoleon suffered defeat in 1814, Pius returned to Rome from France.

Despite these disastrous events, the papacy soon enjoyed a return to authority and even prestige, perhaps surprisingly. As Europe recovered from revolution and Napoleon, so too did the papacy regain new strength. As a result of the Congress of Vienna (1814–1815), which restored many of the civil government structures predating the French Revolution and the Napoleonic age that followed, the papacy again took control of its papal states in central Italy.

The Old World diplomat Joseph de Maistre wrote to support the idea of the papacy as a monarchy. His 1819 treatise on the pope included sentiments that captured the spirit of papal restoration:

> Thousands of times have [the papacy's] enemies reproached us with the weaknesses, the vices even, of those by whom it has been occupied. They did not reflect that every sovereignty must be viewed as a single individual, having possessed all the good and all the bad qualities that belonged to the entire dynasty, and that the succession of popes, thus considered in regard to its general merit, surpasses all others without difficulty and beyond comparison.

But, de Maistre added, the papacy was not just another monarchy.

> The sovereign pontiffs will, ere long, be proclaimed the supreme agents of civilization, the creators of European monarchy and unity, the preservers of the arts and sciences, the founders, the natural protectors of civil liberty, the destroyers of slavery, the enemies of despotism, the indefatigable sustainers of sovereignty, the benefactors of mankind.[5]

One final force was at work during this period that would affect the papacy: nationalism. The nineteenth century saw an upsurge in national identity, language, and culture. Countries began to focus not on what united them, such as the Christian faith that transcends geographic borders, but on their national or ethnic heritage that made them unique. This movement challenged the papacy because nationalism competed with religion as a claim on a person's ultimate allegiance: to the faith or to a particular country. At the same time, this movement also in a sense freed the Church from the political authority that had sometimes handicapped her, as Gallicanism had done. The papacy gradually lost its hold as a temporal power as the Italian unification movement gained speed and nipped away at the independence of the papal states. So the papacy had recourse to a higher authority. The popes emphasized a religious allegiance that crossed the northern Italian Alps—and this led to the word "ultramontanism" (beyond the mountains). In this way the papacy tried to reclaim its hold on a Catholic's ultimate loyalty. At the end of a rough few centuries for the papacy, the ground was beginning to shift toward the strong assertion of ultramontanism and, especially, the question of papal infallibility.

The Modern Church: A World Leader

Ironically, the supposed deathblow to the papacy—the loss of the pope's role as a temporal ruler over the papal states—turned out to be a blessing. As the papacy gradually lost its civil power and prestige in the second half of the nineteenth century and the first half of the twentieth century, popes could focus more on their moral leadership in a rapidly changing world. As the papal historian Eamon Duffy put it elegantly, during the modern era, the popes had become the oracles of God and leaders of a world that was truly "catholic"—universal.

This part of the papal story is closely tied up with the mid-nineteenth-century Italian unification movement called the *Risorgimento,* led by Garibaldi, Mazzini, and King Victor Emmanuel II. At first, Pope Pius IX favored some political reforms and tentative steps toward political participation in Italy, including his own papal states. But when violent social and political revolts swept across Europe in 1848, monarchs including Pius IX reacted strongly against these democratizing measures.

As the papacy's power as a monarch diminished, its appeal "over the mountains" (ultramontanism) grew. The pope saw himself more and more as a leader who was not bound by geography, ethnicity, or nationalism. Pius IX's attention thus switched to a defense of his authority as pope and his role in defending the faith against what he considered scholarly encroachments. These were like leftovers or developments of Enlightenment rationalism and secularism that were now being applied to Catholicism. In 1864, to defend the faith against certain of these tendencies (as they were sometimes called), Pius IX issued the *Syllabus of Errors.* He said, in effect, that Catholics should not embrace some modern ideas, including the very notion that Church and society were compatible and, indeed, could even live in harmony, with each side contributing something good to the other. This negative assessment sounds strange in light of Vatican II's embrace of these very ideas, but Vatican II was still more than a century away. The *Syllabus* denounced rationalism, secularism, materialism, the idea that Catholicism should be only one of several religions protected by the state, and even freedom of religion.

Pius IX also worked toward a definition of papal infallibility and supremacy at Vatican I (1869–1870), the first general council to be held in St. Peter's Basilica. After quite a debate, during which about sixty bishops departed from Rome because they did not want to vote against the doctrine laying down the infallibility of the pope's teaching authority—especially with the pope sitting right there in the council—Vatican I approved the decree. When the pope teaches *ex cathedra* on a matter of faith and morals, his teaching authority is infallible.

Pius IX, the longest serving pope in history (after Peter's traditional thirty-five years as head of the Church), was followed by a very different man. Leo XIII (1878–1903) was very much an Italian aristocrat and monarch, but he was also open to many of the scholarly developments in archaeology, Church history, theology, and biblical studies that Pius IX had opposed. Leo XIII opened the Vatican's archives and pushed people to see Christ in the world around them and to work for change—a movement known as social Catholicism that lit up twentieth-century Catholicism like one of Edison's new light bulbs.

Just as Leo XIII took the papacy in a new direction after Pius IX's thirty-two-year reign, so too did Leo XIII's successor, Pius X (1903–1914), move his own papacy away from Leo's quarter century of developments. Pius X picked up where his namesake, Pius IX, left off. He condemned a list of errors similar to

Pius IX's *Syllabus* and allowed seminaries to be purged of "modernist" professors, often by anonymous accusers. And like everyone else in the first half of the twentieth century, popes were challenged by two world wars. For the papacy, this has manifested itself in the worst case through an ongoing series of charges, defense, countercharges, and counter-defenses about the role that the Church, and especially Pius XII (1939–1958), did or did not play in helping or not helping Jews during the Holocaust.

The twentieth-century papacy also fostered some of the theological and spiritual openness that led to Vatican II. Pius X fought the modernists, but he also encouraged people to receive Holy Communion frequently, even every day. Pius XII was known as an austere and strict man, but he gave strong support to the liturgical renewal that increased the active participation of the faithful in Mass and led eventually to liturgies in vernacular languages. John XXIII (1958–1963) called Vatican II and, in its opening session, roundly criticized "prophets of doom" who were trying to stifle the council before it even got started.

John XXIII, Paul VI (1963–1978), and John Paul II (1978–2005) have each put their mark on the papacy and the Church. John XXIII, in his short, supposedly caretaker papacy, reoriented the fundamental way the Church thought about the world, herself, her leaders, her fellow Christians, and people of other faiths. Paul VI may be called the first global pope—in fact, he was the first pope since Peter to have been in the Holy Land. John Paul II, with over 100 trips outside Italy, energized the world while, by using the media, making it a smaller place. Under John Paul II, the papacy became as centralized, unified, and organized as it has ever been, perhaps to the envy of medieval popes like Gregory VII and Innocent III who had just this sort of prominence in mind. Some criticize his approach, of course, and say he made the world too Roman and too centralized. On the other hand, he was a major player in world events, helping to destroy Communism and to work toward healing centuries of Christian animosity toward Jews. At John Paul II's own urging, theologians and historians have been publicly debating the pope's role. But it is clear that the papacy remains a preeminent institution on the world and religious stage—a far cry from Peter the fisherman, perhaps, but still a line of continuity that can be drawn across every year of Church history in a very unique way.

Chapter 4

DOCTRINE

How did doctrine develop?

Before we start the discussion of how doctrine was formulated and reformulated over the centuries, we must reiterate the idea of development. When we say that doctrine "develops," we do not mean that a belief was not true or did not exist before the Church made an official statement on a particular matter. For instance, Jesus was fully human and fully divine from the moment of his conception in Mary's womb. But the Church did not formulate and agree on the words to describe this mystery until the councils of the fourth and fifth centuries came up with the creeds repeated each Sunday at Mass, "We believe in one God...." It's simply a matter of human beings in different centuries and changing contexts using a variety of languages plus emerging theological vocabularies and methods to catch up to divine mysteries that, ultimately, can never adequately be put into human words. To be clear: the mysteries don't develop, but the words used to express those mysteries in "doctrinal" or "dogmatic" statements do.

The Early Church: Slow and Careful Steps

Without doubt, the early Church's primary theological concern was on explaining who God the Father, Son, and Spirit are individually and in relationship with each other in the Trinity. How could three be one? How could Jesus be divine and human: was he half human and half divine? What was his relationship to his mother and Father? Was he two people: one human and one divine? Did the Spirit come from the Father or the Son—or Father and Son? Was one Person in the Trinity subordinate to the other two?

As the Church moved from groups of believers waiting for Jesus to return to a more structured association of communities strung across the Mediterranean basin, various questions emerged. This was largely because Christianity's essential beliefs—the *kerygma*—had to be passed along to prospective Christians as the faith spread. Even the essential facts of the Easter events—Jesus' death and resurrection—had to be explained to pagans who couldn't accept that God could become human without losing divinity. These explanations varied in their accuracy, and gradually bishops in different locations corresponded with each other to ask how each was dealing with this or that question or explanation. Through this process, both orthodoxy and heresy developed.

Doctrine developed from questions. For instance, an early Christian named Marcion (ca. 85–160) misunderstood Jesus' existence as man and God because he could not understand how evil could exist in the world. Marcion believed there were two gods (dualism): one was good (the Father of Jesus) and the other was bad. The latter created the world, including evil. Marcion believed that Jesus could not have truly been a man because the world and material objects were evil. This idea, later known as docetism (from the Greek "to seem"), claimed that God only seemed or appeared to become human in Jesus. Therefore, Jesus had not really been born of a woman, had not truly died, and did not in fact come back from the dead—which created obvious problems for salvation history.

Another group of people wondered how God's "three-ness" in the Trinity related to God's "one-ness" as Father, Son, and Spirit, each separate from the other. This question led to a series of positions, which were ultimately labeled heretical. One was called "modal monarchianism" and held that, at any one time, God was never three but only one "mode" at a time: God was Father (not Son or Spirit), and then Son (not Father or Spirit), and then Spirit (not Father or Son). "Adoptionism" claimed the Father adopted the human Jesus and raised him to divinity, but the Son's divinity was inferior to the Father's. Arianism said Jesus was never divine, but only a sort of super-human. Arius, a priest in Alexandria in the early fourth century, believed Jesus was neither co-eternal with, nor equal to, the Father. Jesus had followed at a later date and had been "made" by the Father, so he was therefore somehow inferior to the Father, which linked with adoptionism. Arius spoke about Jesus this way: "There was a time when he was not." This position meant the Spirit was all the more "made" by Father (and/or Son) and inferior to both. Once again, trouble with Arianism arose when it came to salvation: if Jesus is not God, then humans are not saved since only God can save.

With all of these questions and answers competing with each other, the churches had to come together and make a definitive statement. Christians could not do this, however, while Christianity remained illegal under the pagan Roman emperors. But with the emergence of the Roman Emperor Constantine and his toleration of Christianity starting in 313, bishops and thinkers could meet to settle the questions. Constantine's meeting, the first of the Church's twenty-one general councils, met in Nicaea, in modern-day Turkey, in 325. There, a deacon named Athanasius refuted Arius. Asked "How is the Son equal to the Father?" Athanasius replied, "Like the sight of two eyes." The bishops agreed to state that Jesus is "begotten, not made" and is "one in being with the Father" (the key Greek word is rendered in English letters as *homoousious*) as well as the Father's equal. The second general council, which met at Constantinople (today's Istanbul) in 381, applied the same concept to the Holy Spirit. The council said that the Spirit, too, was of the same being as Father and Son; that Father, Son, and Spirit were co-eternal; and all three persons of the Trinity were equal. There was never a time, in other words, when the Spirit or Son were not in equal co-existence with the Father.

As often happens, new answers led to new questions, which in turn led to competing ideas that had to be sifted by the Church's authorities. Nestorius (ca. 381–451) taught that Mary had been the mother of the human Jesus, but not the mother of God. Others who followed him claimed that Jesus had been two separate persons, one human (the Son of Mary) and one divine (the Son of God)—the catch phrase was "other and other." This led to more questions: was Jesus human sometimes and God at other times? If so, can we distinguish when he was which during different Gospel scenes? Again, a council helped: Ephesus in 431 declared Nestorianism a heresy and stated clearly that

Jesus has two natures (human and divine) joined in one person by a "hypostatic union." Mary was indeed the Mother of God (*Theotokos*).

Still, doctrinal issues kept arising: "monophysitism" (meaning "one nature") held that Jesus' divine nature swallowed his human nature. This position had roots dating back about a hundred years earlier when a theologian named Apollinarius had fought Arianism by overemphasizing Jesus' divinity. Whereas Arius had said Jesus was never divine, Apollinarius claimed Jesus was so divine that his divinity overtook his humanity. It took the fourth general council, Chalcedon in 451, to explain that, in Jesus, the divine nature became personally united with the human nature, without either the human or the divine nature canceling the other out. Chalcedon countered two centuries of doctrinal missteps (dualism, docetism, adoptionism, modal monarchianism, Arianism, Apollinarianism, Nestorianism, and monophysitism) to sum up Christian doctrine four centuries after the resurrection. Jesus is one person with two natures (human and divine), neither of which dominates the other. Mary is indeed the Mother of God. The Trinity is made up of three Persons—Father, Son, and Spirit—each of whom is co-equal, co-eternal, and of the same being with the other.

The First Millennium Church: A Holding Pattern

THE SIX HUNDRED YEARS BETWEEN the early Church's first four councils and the medieval explosion of theology were not the brightest, but some efforts were made that helped maintain the faith more than expand doctrine. Some of this maintaining took place in monastic libraries and schools. While not functioning as university-level schools, they did act as places where doctrines, especially the writings of the Fathers and the decisions of Church councils, were handed down.

Monastic theology was fairly conservative: it did not concern itself with speculation that might stretch the bounds of orthodoxy. Instead, it "conserved" or "preserved" the early Church's teachings, out of respect for the authority of Scripture and the Fathers. Abbots taught the faith as it was received, not challenged. Learning doctrine was closely related to monastic spirituality, with about twenty hours each week devoted to study and prayerful reading. A lived experience of God entailed community living, prayer, work, and a quest for truth and understanding the things of God. This approach lined up with patristic theology, which recognized the limits of human understanding and language. Council fathers, theologians, and bishops in the earlier period tried to say as little as possible about God because they knew that words really can't describe divine mysteries. In the rest of the first millennium, the goal was preserving those explanations, not expanding them. So the monastic schools taught the basics of reading and writing as training for copying, prayer, and liturgy. Consequently, there was a general distrust of too much analysis or excessive discussion; the concern was that verbal battles and semantics could distract the Christian from doctrinal and spiritual mysteries.

The goal was not an inflated ego or cleverness. Monks and nuns studied to seek God, not to speculate about God.

Some notable examples of this kind of preservation stand out. Boethius (480–524) and Cassiodorus (ca. 490–580) in Italy acted as bridges between the early and medieval Church. Boethius translated parts of Plato and Aristotle's works from Greek to Latin. These works were "rediscovered" in the Middle Ages, with theologians in medieval universities using them to apply pagan principles to Christian doctrine. Boethius' Latin translation of Aristotle's writings on logic, for example, gave medieval theology a system of breaking questions down into key terms, categories, and propositions for analysis. Boethius was preserving the philosophical methodology that became the prerequisite for medieval doctrinal development, which is why philosophy came to be known as the "handmaiden of theology" in the Middle Ages.

Cassiodorus established a monastery in southern Italy where monks copied the great works of antiquity. He himself wrote a book detailing what sort of theological education a monk should have. Like Augustine, Cassiodorus thought Christians should draw from the methods (though not the content) of pagan learning and education. They applied the classical Greco-Roman system of education—the *trivium* (logic, grammar, rhetoric) and *quadrivium* (arithmetic, geometry, astronomy, music)—to Scripture, liturgy, and theology. This approach offered a method for the Middle Ages by demonstrating how words and allegories in

Scripture are signs that must be interpreted and then taught as guidelines for moral living. Theologians and bishops must know original languages as well as the methods of grammar, rhetoric, and reason to comprehend speeches and doctrinal statements; music to sing psalms and celebrate the liturgy; arithmetic to interpret the many numeric symbols in Scripture; and astronomy to calculate feast days.

A Spanish bishop named Isidore of Seville (ca. 570–636) didn't write original commentaries, but he gathered together court decisions and theological and scientific writings that were built upon in subsequent centuries. He also compiled books that listed the Church's teachings on doctrinal issues, such as Christology, and morality. Compilations like these were called *florilegia*—something like little bouquets. While not containing original thinking, they provided the raw material that medieval theologians would analyze and synthesize into books on specific doctrinal topics or themes. In the next centuries, these would be called sentences (*sententiae*) and summaries (*summae*).

What about doctrine proper during these centuries? Even after the flurry of activity in the first four general councils, doctrinal questions kept coming. A second Council of Constantinople met in 553 to reiterate that Nestorianism and monophysitism were heresies. Constantinople II reaffirmed the hypostatic union and all prior conciliar teachings on the Trinity, Christology, and Mary. Now that doctrine on these matters had been settled, the bishops stressed that anyone holding these positions, teaching them, or permit-

ting others to hold or teach them should be condemned. But a final question still arose: how many wills
did Jesus have? Preliminary discussions were held
throughout the spreading world of Christianity—as far
away as England—and opinions were gathered for discussion at the council. Constantinople III in 680–681
decided against the "monothelitists" who taught that
Jesus had only one will. The bishops declared that Jesus'
human nature had one will and his divine nature had
another will.

Despite six general councils, heresies like Arianism
appeared sporadically in northern Europe. From the
late 700s to the early 900s, versions of adoptionism
resurfaced in Spain, though curiously the heresy was
turned around and now held that Jesus' humanity and
not his divinity had been adopted. This version spread
through Europe, leading a synod of bishops meeting in
Frankfurt to condemn adoptionism once again in 794.

Theologians also turned their attention to other
areas of doctrine. For example, many discussed
Augustine's late-fourth and early-fifth-century teachings on grace and free will, with some theologians
emphasizing one over the other. One ninth-century
writer named Gottschalk seemed to say that Christians
are definitely predestined to do either good or evil and
therefore to end up in heaven or hell. An Irish philosopher, John Scotus Erigena (ca. 810–877), opposed
Gottschalk's position, saying that we are all predestined
to act for the good. We may, through failures in free
will, do evil, but God does not predetermine that we
will act for the bad. However, a sufficient theological

vocabulary and methodology had not yet developed to purse this matter very deeply during this period (although the issues of grace, free will, and predestination would become very important doctrinal debates during the Reformations).

Change was coming. Doctrinal vocabulary and methodology would build slowly as a result of emerging schools that would eventually turn into the cathedral schools and then universities of the Middle Ages. Starting in the later 600s, bishops established schools for bright young men to learn doctrine and the other skills necessary to celebrate the sacraments, to teach, and to preach. Some of the best of these were in England. In central Europe, meanwhile, Merovingian and then Carolingian royalty set up small study centers; a king's library held as much religious material as it did "civil." By the time the first millennium turned, the stage was set for universities to arise from these building blocks.

The Medieval Church: Theological Renaissance

MEDIEVAL THEOLOGIANS HELPED DOCTRINE develop because of a radical new way of "doing" theology called scholastic theology. In the medieval centuries, theologians catalogued, synthesized, analyzed, and presented doctrine in the most coherent, organized, systematic, and technical way yet seen in Church history.

Scholastic theology was very different from monastic theology. While monastic theology of the first millennium had been "conservative" and readily deferred to mystery, scholastic theology was more aggressive, assertive, inquisitive, and speculative—sometimes to a fault. It gave a greater role to human reason, logic, and "scientific" processes. Consequently, it could easily cross the line of humility that monks had respected: cleverness or even arrogance sometimes carried the scholastic's day. At worst, this tendency to show off how much a theologian knew or could speculate on was called toward the end of the Middle Ages *sophismata*. It was a kind of sophistry that carries the negative connotations of the word *scholasticism*. Over time, this type of speculation often missed the whole point of theology, which is a pastoral science, and distanced itself from the humanism at the heart of monastic theology. This humanism also drove the emerging scholastics. Indeed, scholastic theology at first often dealt with the most practical pastoral issues: questions concerning marriage, for instance, make up some of the earliest work in doctrine and canon law tackled by scholastic theologians.

The first significant break with monastic theology came with Anselm of Canterbury (ca. 1033–1109), who in *Cur Deus Homo* (*Why God Became Man*) set out to prove that God exists and to demonstrate why God had to become human in order to save human beings. Anselm did not abandon faith and still had the humility of both humanism and monastic theology in mind. He started from a position of faith in order to understand doctrine. This position is expressed in Latin by the famous phrase *fides quaerens intellectum*: faith seeking understanding. The theologian Peter Abelard (1079–1142) added to this methodology more aggressively by lining up contradictory statements of doctrine and raising questions about which was correct in his appropriately titled treatise *Sic et Non* (*Yes and No*). As he put it, "By doubting, we come to inquiry. Through inquiring, we perceive the truth." Abelard had the same goal as Gratian, who produced the era's most well-known synthesis of confusing, competing, and contradictory legal decisions and doctrinal statements. His work, which appeared in 1140, is usually called the *Decretum* for short, but its full title makes the practical point of scholastic theology much more clearly: *A Concordance of Discordant Canons.*

Doctrine needed just this kind of tune-up after more than a thousand years of thinking, arguing, speculating, deciding, raising new questions, letting some answers sit, and revisiting old ideas with fresh words and concepts. Abelard and Gratian's method was quickly codified in formal steps of reasoning that were applied to any number of doctrinal issues. First, a theologian raised a question, for instance, whether (*utrum*) angels had bodies. Then, he listed and explained the arguments, reasons, and precedents against this position by stating "it does not seem that..." (*videtur quod non...*). Next, he deliberately took the exact opposite stance: "but against this..." (*sed contra est...*). Next, he made a decision about the two prior steps, reconciled opposing ideas, and declared his position: "I respond that..." (*respondeo*). Finally, he listed his responses to any further objections that he thought might be raised against his position: "against the first point...and the second point..." (*ad primum...ad secundum...*). It wasn't long before questions were gathered together by theme, and new genres appeared to discuss doctrine: a *summa* was a large collection that treated a subject comprehensively (Eucharist, other sacraments, marriage, morality, the Trinity), while a *quodlibet* was a short opinion on a particular matter, typically a controversial contemporary debate.

This methodology found a home in the medieval universities that had grown from the bishops' schools and other study centers of earlier centuries. Regulations from the general councils Lateran III (1179) and Lateran IV (1215) mandated that money be set aside in each cathedral community for teachers in the *trivium* (grammar, rhetoric, logic) and theology to train priests to study Scripture and care for their parishioners. These schools held the seeds of university structures and positions, since they had to have deans in charge, archivists and librarians, and teachers and students. Increasingly from the twelfth century on, university communities flourished in Bologna, Oxford and Cambridge, Paris, and elsewhere throughout Europe. Syllabi and curricula soon became standardized, tuitions were negotiated, and teachers and students formed guilds. After a basic arts education of five or six years that began at age fourteen, students specialized in theology, law, or medicine for another dozen years (if they stayed all the way for their "doctorate").

Of course, Thomas Aquinas (ca. 1225–1274) is the superstar of medieval scholastic theology. Like his colleagues, he benefited from the revival of the study of Aristotle's thought on politics, logic, and ethics, which had been preserved by Muslims, Christians, and Jews.

Across the Middle East and North Africa, Muslims had translated Greek sources into Arabic; in Spain (especially Toledo), some of these Arabic sources were in turn translated into Hebrew and Latin. Because of trading contacts with Muslims in the Mediterranean, this material began to have a strong impact in Spain, Sicily, and Italy.

Aquinas' *Summa Theologiae* is the most well-known attempt to reconcile the Church's traditional writings with this rediscovered Greek vocabulary, philosophy, and principles, but there were many *summae* written during the Middle Ages. Thomas was not afraid to apply pagan principles to Christian doctrine, since he had such great confidence in Catholic truth. Nor did he think we should fear where our intellects and reason would take us. Aquinas knew that God was ultimately a mystery beyond human genius—even his own: after he had a heavenly vision, Aquinas tried to destroy everything he'd written about doctrine.

Another movement called nominalism flourished around 1350–1500. Nominalists were often concerned with the doctrine of salvation. They built on some of the darker aspects of Augustinian thought and emphasized man's tendency to act poorly because of sin and lust. Because we are not as good as we ought to be, some nominalists said, we need grace and justification for our salvation. No Christian would argue that point, but nominalists held that grace and justification come much more from God rather than from any human efforts. In retrospect this makes nominalism seem like a slippery slope toward the salvation theories of Luther and especially Calvin, who spoke about predestination in the Reformation era that followed.

The Reformation Church: Getting Back on Track

In the late medieval period, the negative aspects of *sophismata* and scholasticism dominated doctrinal discussions. But even before Luther, a significant number of bishops, theologians, professors, and university leaders were complaining that doctrine had become divorced from pastoral, practical consequences. Too many theologians were ignoring the essentials of preaching, teaching, and spreading the faith. Instead, they argued about tiny details in a kind of parlor game to show off their knowledge. Scholastic theology had devolved into cold lists of reasons why a position was right or wrong and had lost its purpose of moral guidance.

Because doctrine had lost its way, humanists like Erasmus, along with Luther and other Protestant reformers, asked fundamental questions, just as the early Church had done. What were the primary texts and languages on which doctrine had been constructed? What was the point of certain Church beliefs and actions? Had some of the original meanings and intents of doctrine been lost in the later Middle Ages? What were the moral implications of doctrine? What is Jesus' role in salvation? What is the human's place in the world, in salvation, and in relationship with God? What authority does Scripture have? Who judges doctrine? How should the Church be organized? In fact, Luther and Erasmus would write opposing books on the core issue of free will, which demonstrates that Christians from a variety of perspectives were trying to get doctrine back on track.

Protestant and Catholic answers to these questions produced competing doctrines. Doctrines are of course highly nuanced and complex, but we can say basically that Luther was primarily concerned with grace and justification. This makes sense since he was trained as an Augustinian monk and would have read deeply in Augustine's fairly pessimistic writings on sin, free will, and grace. Luther strongly emphasized God's role in salvation and did not see any inherent merit in human action alone when it came to justification. For him, then, the Catholic system of sacraments and indulgences was not only tainted by excess, but largely unnecessary for salvation. Calvin went further by teaching that, from the moment of their creation, humans are destined to heaven or hell (double predestination). As for the related idea of original sin, Protestants held a variety of ideas. Most of these reached back to the fourth-century thought of Pelagius. His idea that Adam's sin stained only himself had been declared a heresy, which Augustine fought. Likewise, some Protestants taught that Adam's sin tainted only himself, while others went a little beyond that to say that he also set a bad example for others, although he did not pass along original sin to the rest of the human race.

Led by Luther and Calvin, the Protestants saw many elements of the Catholic sacramental and devotional systems as additions that came after the New Testament and early Church. Luther felt that these additions were not authentic. He sought a return to the first few centuries of Christianity, before Constantine favored the Church with protection and patronage. In terms of the nature and structure of the Church (the branch of theology called ecclesiology), Protestants saw in the early Church a horizontal arrangement of power. These perspectives deleted years of doctrinal developments that were part of Catholicism's organic tradition, legitimate growth, and vertical/hierarchical ecclesiology, especially concerning the papacy and the College of Cardinals.

Protestant challenges created the need for greater clarity and synthesis concerning Catholic doctrine. The Council of Trent (1545–1563) answered these questions, producing a kind of response-reaction to doctrinal development that reminds us of the question-and-response cycle of the first general councils concerning Christology, Trinitarian theology, and Mariology. Scholars call this development "positive theology," which was the older, original scholastic theology stripped of the silliness of scholasticism and *sophismata*. Positive theology focused on explaining Roman Catholic doctrine versus Protestant doctrines (specifically about Scripture, Tradition, and the sacraments) both in terms of the original sources and legitimate development. These theologians tried to avoid scholasticism and make statements that were clear, pastorally oriented, and comprehensible.

Trent reemphasized the importance of Scripture and its correct interpretation by qualified authorities. The council stated that Tradition (the teachings of the Fathers, conciliar and papal statements, creeds, and other authoritative decisions) partnered with Scripture are the twin poles of Church teaching and authority. When it came to doctrines concerning salvation, justification, and grace, Catholics did not exclude the important role of human actions in collaboration with Jesus' indisputable work of salvation through his passion. Trent reaffirmed the need for human action and the role of free will, while recognizing Jesus' essential and indispensable role in salvation. The council rejected predestination (and double predestination, at that) and stated that Adam's sin was in fact transmitted to all other human beings. We are therefore born with original sin that must be cleansed through Baptism. This sacrament makes a real change in a person's life and is not simply a symbolic introduction to Christianity.

The bishops declared clearly what the seven sacraments are and explained why they are sacraments. They explained all the sacraments, but especially noted that the Eucharist is the Real Presence of Jesus that occurs during a process called *transubstantiation*. This scholastic word had first been used at a general council, Lateran IV, in 1215. Here we find a good example of how scholastic theology's categories and vocabulary bubbled up into official doctrine. This scholastic word allowed the Church to explain more precisely how the bread and wine are truly and completely transformed into Jesus' real body and blood although the bread and wine appear to remain. This teaching stood against a variety of Protestant beliefs about the "Lord's Supper," as it was commonly called in

Protestant theology. Such beliefs included consubstantiation (bread and wine remain and coexist with Jesus' body and blood) and the idea of memorial alone, in which the bread and wine never change at all and simply symbolize Jesus' body and blood.

Once Catholic doctrine had been reaffirmed and restated, apologists spread these teachings, sometimes in a combative or controversial way. On the Catholic side, the best example of this approach comes from the Jesuit Robert Bellarmine (1542–1621). His work, *The Controversies,* was a kind of Catholic textbook used to refute Protestant doctrines. His catechism, translated into more than sixty languages, was carried by missionaries around the globe until the twentieth century. More gently, Jesuits and other theologians, particularly missionaries in Spain and in the territories that would be called South and Latin America, tried to recapture the pastoral aspects of scholastic theology and humanism.

Starting with Trent and continuing via catechisms, sermons, and classes, theologians and catechists always used Scripture, Church history, canon law, and the councils to explain what authentic Catholic doctrine is and how it developed legitimately over time. Study of doctrine was also emphasized: the Jesuit program of study called the *Ratio Studiorum* mandated that every Jesuit school have a library budget so Jesuits would not go out into the world as "unarmed soldiers." Peter Canisius (1521–1597), a Jesuit who worked hard in Germany to reclaim areas to Catholicism, declared bluntly that he would rather have a school without a church than without a library. Doctrine was back on track.

The Early Modern Church: Explaining the Faith to a Changing World

IN THE CENTURIES AFTER THE Council of Trent ended in 1563, the Church devoted her energy to promoting its agenda: revitalizing catechesis and clarifying doctrine in light of competing Protestant theology. This effort did not result in the development of new doctrine. Instead, it emphasized positive theology, moral theology, and apologetics (sometimes called "controversial theology"), which were designed to describe and, if necessary, defend Catholic doctrine. Greater attention was paid to explaining and proselytizing than to expanding doctrine. Demonstrations and presentations of dogma appeared more frequently than discussions, in part because Catholics were still competing with Protestants.

In previous eras, moral theology had typically been integrated with other doctrines. But in this period treatises and catechetics focused more directly on giving moral guidance so that people would know how to live their Christian lives in accordance with Catholic doctrine. It's not that anything new was said, but morality was presented in a fresher, clearer, easier to understand way, and it was now set apart from other branches of theology. As a result of these directions and goals—as well as slowly increasing literacy rates—Catholic doctrine began to appear more frequently than ever before in encyclopedias, catechisms, manuals, and lists of "proof texts." These sources first stated Catholic doctrines and then showed where they came from by citing Scripture, conciliar statements, and theological treatises. Books and pamphlets, particularly on moral theology, were written in a style and at a level aimed especially for the European masses and the indigenous populations that missionaries met in the Far East and the Americas. Above all, the Church's authority to teach doctrine, recognize error, and regulate conduct was affirmed repeatedly.

During this period, however, two related Catholic doctrinal movements veered into heresy: Jansenism and Quietism. Both returned to longstanding questions: What is the human being's relationship with God? Where did grace and free will come into play within that relationship? Jansenism again drew on Augustine's pessimism that said people tended to act poorly when motivated by lust and greed. Jansenism laid too great an emphasis on the sinfulness of human beings. Following a bishop and theologian named Cornelius Jansen (1585–1638) and his book *Augustinus* (published posthumously in 1640), Jansenists believed human beings had been born with justice, but then lost it in the Fall. Christ restored that justice and therefore effected our redemption, but remarkably Jansen held that this action was still not enough for salvation. People needed additional grace to fight their evil tendencies, he said, and taught that not everyone gets this extra grace from God. Jansen was not a Calvinist, however, because he believed humans who receive this grace must cooperate with God through their good works. But Jansen did come close to predestination in his notion of the elect and nonelect, which denied the Catholic doctrine that everyone can be saved.

Jesuit scholastic humanists were also writing on these topics, but they took a more optimistic approach. The Jansenists sometimes accused them of being too lax when it came to pronouncing on human sin and culpability in moral theology. In response, the Jesuits labeled the Jansenists "rigorists." The Jesuits stressed the Catholic doctrine that Christ provided "sufficient grace" through his passion for humanity's redemption. Apart from differences in fundamental theology, in practical terms the conflict between Jesuits and Jansenists might come down to this: if a person thought he *might* have sinned, the Jesuit would allow him to receive the Eucharist, but the Jansenist would forbid receiving. It should come as no surprise that two popes condemned Jansenism: Innocent X in 1653 and Clement XI in 1713.

Quietism saw human beings as extremely passive in their relationship with God. It came close to Protestant doctrine by denying that good works played an important role in a human being's salvation. Quietists recommended long periods of very quiet prayer in which Christians abandoned themselves to God and waited passively to receive insight or revelations. Quietism also deemphasized the role of the intellect in contemplating God. It wasn't long before Quietists were rejecting good works, traditional devotions, and even some sacraments. This was another reason for them to be labeled as Protestants, since the most marked characteristic of this age was to reiterate what is and isn't Catholic doctrine.

About the same time, romanticism brought the Middle Ages back in vogue in terms of art, architecture,

literature, and religion. Romanticism was something of
a reaction to the perceived coldness, pure rationalism,
and deism (if not the occasional outright atheism) of
the Scientific Revolution and the Enlightenment.
Romanticism led to a certain historical albeit flawed
consciousness. Early modern romantics tended to see
the medieval Church with proverbial rose-colored
glasses: a civilization completely unified, with Church
and state molded seamlessly and without conflict into
one idealistic Christian world where theology and secular matters merged perfectly. The conflict between
romanticism and the Enlightenment ebbed and flowed.
John Locke wrote a treatise called the *Reasonableness of
Christianity* in 1695 that kept *fides* and *intellectum* in balance. But often enough raw empiricism replaced *fides
quaerens intellectum* to claim that faith and belief in revelation and miracles were unnecessary or—worse—
implausible, ignorant, superstitious, silly, and abhorrent
to a scientific mindset. Original sin made no sense to
Enlightenment *philosophes,* who returned to the classic
questions of how evil could exist in a world created by
a benevolent deity.

The Modern Church: Many Methods, Much Renewal

The most recent 150 years or so of Church history
have witnessed a revival of traditional scholasticism, the
introduction of new methods of doing theology, and
some radical ideas that have met with very mixed
responses. This period of Church history has witnessed,

therefore, an intense and varied period of reexamined and revitalized theology. This theology is often based on scientific methods being applied to doctrine, Church history, liturgy, and Scripture, and is described by the large umbrella phrase *nouvelle théologie*. We've had three major magisterial teachings in the modern Church: the doctrine of the Immaculate Conception (1854), papal infallibility (1870), and the Assumption (1950). Beyond these major statements, the modern era has been one of the richest periods of theology since the Church's first few centuries.

One of the most significant developments was the revival of scholasticism, especially as represented by Thomas Aquinas. We generally call this movement "neo-scholasticism," the "neo-scholastic revival," or "neo-Thomism." Pope Leo XIII's encyclical *Aeterni Patris* (1879), which restored scholastic theology in seminaries, gave a major impetus to this movement. The pope also established the Roman Academy of St. Thomas and another study center devoted to Aquinas in Louvain. He ordered that Aquinas' texts be reedited and declared Aquinas the patron saint of Catholic education. Journals in diverse languages soon focused on Aquinas, with many articles applying the medieval scholastic method to modern questions of philosophy and doctrine. The next pope, Pius X, required that Aquinas' *Summa Theologiae* be the principal theology textbook in all schools, specifically seminaries, that gave pontifical degrees.

Although we have been talking for some time already about the development of doctrine, the theologian who spoke most eloquently about this idea lived at the dawn of modernity. John Henry Newman (1801–1890) went back to the fourth-century Arian controversies to remind Christians that doctrinal definitions will always fall short of God's reality. No phrase, no creed, no treatise can fully capture the essence of revelation, so he reminded Catholics to beware of intellectual arrogance that puts reason ahead of revelation, subjective knowledge before objective truth, and man ahead of God. In many ways, Newman stood against the kind of late medieval scholasticism and *sophismata* that he saw reemerging in Enlightenment rationalism. Newman was dissatisfied with science's focus on change; instead, he pursued the notion of development and the authority needed to decide what developments were in fact authentic. Truth, he said, is unchanging and eternal, but modern science seemed to say that change is the rule and therefore truth could not exist. So Newman looked at the history of doctrine in search of the continuity of religious principles that do not change, even if the words used to describe doctrines had evolved. He saw tradition as something that lived and breathed, but that did not change in its essential truth.

In a sermon he gave in 1839 on "Faith and Reason, Contrasted as Habits of the Mind," Newman explained that faith and reason are very different approaches to knowledge and truth. Speaking in a very scholastic style (proposition, arguments against faith and then in support of faith, objections, resolution of contradictions), Newman reached certain conclusions. He said that while religious assent depends to a certain degree on the probability of a truth and its logic, scientific proof can never lead the heart to real faith. In this way, Newman synthesized the medieval and early modern tension between faith and intellect, pointing the way to a modern theology that embraced new methods while keeping faith and mystery in a central position.

Indeed, the modern Church witnessed theology reborn, in a sense, with new methodologies (some of which were denounced as "modernism"). As the nineteenth century moved into the twentieth, scholars and theologians, especially in France and Germany, used these new methods extensively. They employed Church history, archaeology, and textual analysis of Scripture and many other documents to revisit doctrine and enhance Christian teachings with greater clarity, accuracy, and freshness. They were trying to steer a middle course between the extremes of the Enlightenment and romanticism, especially the idealized Middle Ages. They saw revelation as something dynamic, yet always in dialogue with Tradition. Church history especially helped the theologians and bishops before, during, and after Vatican II to renew liturgy, prayer, spirituality, and ecclesiology. They looked back to the Church's earliest centuries to find the most original and authentic expressions of Christian life, and then sought to update them to the modern world.

Like prior periods, the modern age has offered not new doctrines as much as new ways of looking at traditional beliefs. Vatican II (1962–1965) was not a doctrinal council like Nicaea I or Trent, but a pastoral council that gave shape and authority to various "paradigm shifts" in theology that had been brewing for over a century. These paradigm shifts asked us to look again at key parts of Catholicism, but to use new scholarly and pastoral methods and ideas that reached a certain critical mass at the council and afterward. They also pressed Catholics to understand how doctrine must be applied in practical ways in their families, communities, and workplaces—to engage the world and not shrink from it. As a result, we have had "theologies" of the laity (single, married, parenthood), of the diaconate, of ecclesiology (focusing more on collegiality and shared decision making—known as *communio* ecclesiology), and of the very idea of what we mean by the word "vocation." We have also had theologies that have drawn criticism from the Church's authorities, such as Pope John Paul II's rejection of much of liberation theology from Latin and South America. Surely, much more work needs to be done, particularly on theologies that wake up our understanding, appreciation, and celebration of Confirmation and Penance, as well as of the essential role of women. As always, Catholics must remember that doctrine's development must be aligned with Church history, tradition, and authority if it is to be judged as an authentic expression of truth, while recognizing that no statement of doctrine can ever fully capture the essence of that mysterious truth.

Chapter 5

THE MASS

How did the Mass develop?

The Early Church: Jewish Origins to Sunday Services

PERHAPS THE MOST IDENTIFIABLE way to see Catholics in action liturgically is to attend a Mass, but today's Mass developed to its present form only after much time. The earliest Christians were mostly Jews, so naturally their liturgies developed from Jewish sources. Although the Last Supper was like a Jewish seder, the first Christians began to gradually adapt Jewish rituals to their new faith in Jesus Christ as the Son of God. So, in the first few centuries of Christianity, what we call the Mass began in the context of a shared meal on the Jewish Sabbath of Friday night and participation in the Saturday synagogue services. These were a forerunner of the Liturgy of the Word. But it gradually moved away from these beginnings into its own liturgical service on Sunday morning, the day of Jesus' resurrection.

In the Jewish ritual that Jesus' first followers would have practiced for most of their lives, bread and wine were blessed separately, probably at the beginning of a shared meal. The earliest Christians did this for the few years right after Jesus' death and resurrection. But by the 40s A.D., a little more than a decade later, it appears that bread and wine were blessed together, at the end of a fellowship meal, which was called an *agape*. Moving the ritual to the end of the meal led to something of a separation of the Eucharist (from the Greek word for "giving thanks") from the *agape*. Over time this led to a complete separation of the two events: a meal and a

Eucharist. Today's Mass, however, retains a vestige of the union of Eucharist and *agape:* the offertory represents the time when people would bring food and drink to the combined events.

This separation may have occurred because at the *agape* some Christians drank too much, and divisions led to the unfair distribution of food. Some Christians even went hungry. In the 50s A.D., St. Paul chastised the Corinthians for such scandalous behavior at their gatherings, which should have been the occasion for fellowship and forgiveness (1 Cor 11:17–22). By the end of the first century and the beginning of the second, therefore, the Eucharist and the *agape* had pulled apart. The Eucharist moved to Sunday morning and the meal to Saturday or Sunday evening, but the meal disappeared entirely by the early fourth century. This probably happened because Christians could gather more freely when they wanted after Constantine favored Christianity about that time.

Because the Eucharist was separated from the *agape,* some things were lost: talking, sharing news, hearing directions from leaders, reading out loud Paul's letters or passages from the Gospels, singing— everything that makes a meal a celebration. So, following Jewish examples from synagogue services, on Saturday mornings Christians gathered for a pair of readings from Scripture, a sermon, prayers for aid, and songs. Before long, this Saturday morning service (what we now call the Liturgy of the Word) was moved to and combined with Sunday morning's Liturgy of the Eucharist. Probably within a century after Jesus' time on earth, but surely by the early 200s, we can find a Mass fairly close in structure to the Mass today.

Most of these gatherings were celebrated in Greek, the language of the people, but the few records that remain show a certain diversity. At the Word liturgy and the Eucharist, there was probably a head table, perhaps raised. There sat the presider, who was usually the man whom we today would call the bishop. Different leaders, however, conducted their services using variations of prayers, readings, and blessings because formulaic prayers and versions of Scripture were not yet codified. The wording of prayers allowed for some freedom, but surely an oral culture that handed important words down orally made certain that the key words of the Eucharist remained as closely uniform as possible. Moreover, some rituals occurred at different times during the liturgy. Christians exchanged the kiss of peace after the intercessions and before the offertory until the fifth century, at which time it was moved to the Eucharist. But during the 300s in North Africa and Rome, Christians kissed after the Eucharistic prayer. We know, too, that Christians received the Eucharist not on their tongues, but in their hands.

By the early third century, however, leaders were urging greater precision in liturgical language and practice, which was important since how Christians pray must match the doctrines they believe. About the year 225, a Christian leader named Hippolytus wrote a manual called *Apostolic Tradition* with texts to be used as a guide. His earliest version of the Eucharistic prayers familiar to us was still in Greek, and it had the intended effect of making the vocabulary of the Eucharist generally more standard. By the early 200s, the liturgies in Rome were in Latin, and by the late 300s, Latin was more common everywhere. As a result, both the Bible, with Jerome's Vulgate (Latin) translation, and liturgical services took on a more formal, standard, and literary tone.

The Mass also developed its own place and time. In 321, the Roman Emperor Constantine made Sunday a holiday. The "Lord's Day" was now a legal day off every week, but Christians had been gathering for over 200 years on that day of Jesus' resurrection. Where did they gather? Within weeks or months after Jesus' resurrection, Jews met in their homes—later called "house churches"—to talk about Jesus. Once the Romans leveled Jerusalem and scattered the Jews into exile (diaspora) in A.D. 70, these house churches sprang up more frequently around the Mediterranean, although they had begun to do so even before Jerusalem fell. When Romans periodically persecuted Christians as pagans and traitors to the empire, Christians met secretly. Rome's catacombs contain frescoes that look like an *agape,* a Eucharist, or perhaps a representation of the heavenly banquet. Under Constantine, the number of Christians grew and house churches could no longer contain them. Church buildings were now legal, so as Christianity developed more freely and legally, so too did the structure and setting of the Mass become more codified.

The First Millennium Church: Growing Standardization

DURING THIS NEXT PERIOD OF CHURCH history, the Mass and other rites grew more standardized, largely through the efforts of the popes and their advisors in Rome. They wanted to ensure that all Christians celebrated the Eucharist in much the same way. Because popes were sending missionaries into Europe to spread the faith to pagans and defend it against heretics, the need arose for a solid and standard way of offering Mass to unify the growing Church.

To achieve this goal of uniformity, the Church began to designate certain texts as the authentic collections of prayers, readings, and rituals that everyone was to follow in order to celebrate Mass properly. Most of these texts and rituals dealt with elaborate liturgies celebrated by popes and bishops, not the simple Mass celebrated by a priest in a small parish. Nevertheless, the centrality of these Roman collections could serve as a starting point and guide, in hopes that a standard liturgy would eventually trickle down into the parishes and unite Christians throughout Europe. In fact, the Synod of Whitby held in 664 mandated that all Christians in the British Isles had to adopt Roman liturgical rites. This applied especially to the Irish, who were dating the celebration of Easter according to a formula different than Rome's.

The most important collections were called sacramentaries, which were gathered together under the names of several popes, including Leo I (440–461),

Gelasius I (492–496), and Gregory I (590–604). These popes did not always have a direct hand in the sacramentaries that bore their names, but the identification of their names lent prestige and authenticity to these collections, which began to appear in the middle 500s. These sacramentaries included prayers and blessings said on feasts or during liturgical seasons such as Lent and Advent, the prayers said over the gifts of bread and wine, the prayers of consecration, and prayers said before and after Communion. The best of these, attributed generally to Church Fathers, were collected and gradually gained widespread usage.

Groups of readings for the Mass were collected. At first, these collections held only the beginning (*incipit*) and ending (*explicit*) words of the passages to be read, which the priest could use to find the complete selection in his Bible. Later, the full texts of the passages were published in the lectionaries. Some lectionaries contained only Paul's letters (epistolaries) or the Gospels (evangeleries). Collections of hymns and chanted parts of the Mass, called antiphonaries, followed as well. They included the entrance hymn, the *Kyrie,* the *Gloria,* the Gradual (psalm verse after the first reading—what we call the responsorial psalm), the *Credo,* the *Sanctus,* the *Agnus Dei,* and the closing statement *Ite, missa est* ("Go, the Mass is ended"). Sample homilies, often drawn from the Fathers of the Church, were gathered in homiliaries.

To make sure that the Mass was celebrated properly, sometimes directions were written in red ink—from which we get the word *rubric*—in all of these collections, so the Mass celebrant would know what to do when. Some books contained nothing but rubrics. A master of ceremonies often used these books of directions, called *ordines.*

What effect did these collections have on the Mass? From the sixth to the tenth centuries, liturgies became more uniform in the most essential parts of the Mass, such as the consecration, although local variety still existed to serve popular devotions in particular regions. Spain had a Mozarabic rite, which still exists in Toledo, and an Ambrosian rite that continues to flourish in Milan. A generally standard way of celebrating Mass spread to France, up into German lands, and over to Spain, but these countries also influenced liturgy. Christianity found a base north of Rome in the imperial courts of Pepin III (751–768), his son Charlemagne (768–814), and Charlemagne's son, Louis the Pious (814–840). These rulers supplied money and patronage for libraries and study centers where theology and liturgy were codified, copied, and disseminated with papal approval and cooperation.

While the Mass had become more austere, stately, and formal, it also changed and grew. During the seventh century, important additions were made to the Mass, such as the *Kyrie,* the *Agnus Dei,* and the breaking of the Host. These rites and prayers had been included in liturgies celebrated in particular places and gradually became universal. The Creed had been used during baptisms, but not always in Masses, as it was in the East in the sixth century. Under Charlemagne, the Creed was added after the Gospel. From his court in northern Europe, this introduction of the Creed into the Mass spread to Rome. This offers an interesting example of a liturgical change being introduced from Christianity's periphery to her center in Rome and then, from Rome, to the rest of the Church.

These developments had positive and negative aspects. Certainly structure and uniformity were essential to a Church that must celebrate the Mass in substantially the same way and believe the same things theologically. It appears that uniformity in essentials was balanced with diversity in local devotions or practices. This allowed missionaries on Europe's frontiers to bring new believers into the faith without alienating them. Celtic and German songs were transformed into Christian hymns, for instance. As much as Charlemagne wanted liturgical uniformity with Rome, he found that the Roman Mass collections did not include local customs. So he set his favorite scholar Alcuin (735–804) to the task of gathering and adding them for his local bishops and priests.

But gradually, the people no longer actively participated in the liturgy and instead merely watched it happen. Most Christians no longer spoke Latin, but it remained the liturgical language, so many did not always understand the words spoken at the altar. But they could see symbolic dramatizations such as an entrance and Gospel procession, multiple incensations, and anointings during episcopal and royal consecrations. These dramatizations included the parishioners in the Mass, but sometimes distracted them from the centrality of the consecration. Moreover, over time extra-

liturgical practices began to attract more of their attention than the Mass did. This development leads us to
the Middle Ages.

The Medieval Church: Private Masses

THE MIDDLE AGES SAW A VARIETY of devotional practices
that in some cases supported attention to the Mass and
in others diverted it away. While the Middle Ages witnessed a tremendous upsurge in popular devotions, the
central act of people's faith was not always the Mass.
Medieval Christians loved a party and they celebrated
many feast days, especially those devoted to local saints
and Mary, with parades, plays, and fairs. Many of these
holidays allowed Christians to exercise their devotions,
but these did not always include the Mass. Several reasons spurred this development, but the rise of individual Masses dominates this part of Church history.

During the medieval period, the number of Masses
said by individual priests, with no one except a single
altar server in attendance, rose dramatically. This did not
happen because Christians abandoned the Mass, however. In fact, quite the opposite was true: people had
tremendous faith in the power of a Mass offered for a
particular purpose—especially to help someone's soul
advance from purgatory to heaven. They believed that
when more Masses were offered for their intention, the
better the chance that the intention would be fulfilled.
This motivation led people to endow churches and
especially monasteries with gifts of money so Masses
could be offered for one specific purpose: typically, to

pray for one's soul or the soul of a family member (perhaps even in perpetuity) to make sure that God would forgive their sins and allow them to enter heaven. Despite the laudable faith behind this motivation, it led to the loss of several extremely important elements of the Mass: the active participation of the faithful and the exercise of the Mass as a communal—as opposed to an individual—celebration.

These individual or private masses—also known as "dry" or "read" masses—were often stripped to the bare essentials: no hymns, no incensations, no responses from a congregation (which often was not even present), and no interaction between priest and people. More prayers were said by the priest alone. The kiss of peace disappeared among the people. If more than one priest was present, they shared the kiss of peace among themselves alone or simply kissed a plate or paten (on which the Eucharist would rest) and passed it along to the next priest.

Architecture also moved the Mass from a communal to an individual event. In the early Church, the priest and altar faced the people, often in a horseshoe or round setting. Starting slowly in the sixth century, altars had been placed against the church's side walls to supplement the main altar. This enabled as many altars as possible to be crammed into side chapels, to accommodate private masses without a congregation. By 1000, altars placed at the wall and priests standing with their backs to the congregation were the norms. In the larger churches and in basilicas, a "rood screen" sometimes blocked the main altar almost entirely from the people's sight. The Mass had become distanced from the people, who did not even speak its Latin language.

It is not surprising, then, that people rarely received Holy Communion at Mass. When they did, they now received on the tongue, not in the hand, and the chalice was given only to royalty or aristocracy, if at all. People received Communion so infrequently that the Fourth Lateran Council in 1215 had to order Christians to confess their sins and receive the Eucharist once a year, which came to be known as the Easter duty.

This did not mean, however, that people lost faith in the Eucharist. In fact, a great deal of evidence points to the contrary: people had such a reverence for the Eucharist that they did not think they measured up to receiving Communion more than once a year. We know of the esteem for the Eucharist from two main sources. First, elevations of the Eucharist became important moments in the Mass. When many Masses were being said in side-by-side altars set along the main bodies of large churches and basilicas, parishioners would move from one altar to the next, crying "Higher" at the elevation so they could see the Eucharist. Masses were sometimes begun at five-minute intervals just so people could move from one altar to the next when they heard the altar server ring a little bell to signal the next elevation. Second, Corpus Christi processions were wildly popular during the Middle Ages, with elaborate floats and celebrations marking the movement of the Eucharist, displayed in a monstrance, through the town square. Some of this—

along with morality and Passion plays, veneration of relics, saints' feasts, and rosaries—surely led to devotional excesses at times devoid of complete understanding of the Real Presence and other theological points. But it cannot be denied that these actions flowed from a real faith and reverence for the Eucharist.

At the same time, the Masses and rituals of Holy Week were made more elaborate. This also indicated religious devotion even if people were not receiving Communion. Many of these rituals grew because of the rising number of pilgrims and crusaders who had spent time in the Holy Land. There, they witnessed the intricate Holy Week liturgies celebrated at the very places where Jesus suffered, died, was buried, and rose from the dead. They brought these memories home with them, and the clergy who traveled to Bethlehem and Jerusalem learned to incorporate the Holy Land liturgies into European settings. In more and more places in Europe, churches held a procession on Palm Sunday, performed the public washing of feet on Holy Thursday, chanted the Passion and venerated the cross on Good Friday, sang *Tenebrae* and the *Exultet* on Holy Saturday, and celebrated the Easter Vigil by lighting the Easter fire and candles.

Liturgical uniformity and centralization continued during this period as well. Several times in the late eleventh century, Church councils under papal leadership mandated that the Roman rite for celebrating Mass supersede local customs. A century later, in 1172, the Synod of Cashco reiterated the Synod of Whitby's action in 664 that made the Roman rite the rule in the

British Isles. This movement at centralization was fueled by the papacy's desire to free the Church from secular control and to make the Church as catholic or universal as possible while Christianity continued to expand. Some voices, however, soon objected not only to papal centralization, but also to liturgical and devotional excesses, especially private Masses. These criticisms would soon change the course of Church history and lead to a strong defense of just what Catholics believed when they celebrated Mass.

The Reformation Church: Challenge and Response

The various Protestant reformers raised fundamental questions concerning the very nature of the Eucharist—and therefore of how to celebrate the Mass. Was the bread and wine truly transformed into the body and blood of Jesus, with nothing essential of the bread and wine remaining? Did bread and wine remain, but coexist with the body and blood? Was Jesus not present at all, with the bread and wine only symbolizing body and blood? All of these questions affected not only the theology of the Eucharist, but also the celebration of the Mass.

The Protestant critiques of the Mass and the Eucharist can be gathered under two central points, although multiple Protestant reformers held a variety of positions about the Eucharist.

First, Protestants critiqued the Catholics' theology of transubstantiation, a term Catholics use to express their belief that during the consecration, the bread and wine truly and completely become Jesus' actual body and blood in the Eucharist. The Real Presence of Jesus remains in the Eucharist. It does not go away when the congregation disperses, which is why the Eucharist is reserved in a tabernacle. Some Protestants believed in consubstantiation, whereby bread and wine exist along with Jesus' body and blood. Others thought that the event at the altar was only a memorial, not a sacrifice, and the bread and wine never ceased being anything but bread and wine. Jesus, in essence, was present in spirit or memory only. Others said that Jesus existed in the community gathered around the altar to remember his death and resurrection, which brings us to the second aspect of the Protestant critiques.

The Protestant critique was not just of the Eucharist, but of the Mass. The multiplication of dry or private masses had lost the essential connection between priest and people united in one worshipping community in the Real Presence of Jesus in the Eucharist. Some Protestant groups believed that Jesus was present in the bread, but stopped being present once the congregation exited the church building, which is why they did not reserve the bread and wine in a tabernacle. For these Protestants, it would be like putting a simple loaf of bread and bottle of wine in a special place for no reason.

While Catholics, then and now, reject these two critiques, it remains true that Church leaders during the medieval period did not adequately educate people about the Eucharist and Mass. Faced with the

Protestant challenges in this and many other areas of theology and Church organization, the popes and bishops of the Reformation era explicitly emphasized just what the Church does and does not teach about the Eucharist and how she should or should not celebrate Mass. The popes and bishops knew that, during the Middle Ages, the understanding and celebration of the Mass had flagged. To remedy this, the Council of Trent took up this reeducation effort during its sessions from 1545 to 1563.

Trent affirmed transubstantiation, a word first used officially at the Fourth Lateran Council in 1215, when stipulating that Christians must confess their sins and receive Communion once each year. Trent also affirmed the lasting and Real Presence of Jesus in the Eucharist beyond the consecration and the celebration of the Mass. But to make sure that the Mass was celebrated properly both liturgically and theologically, after Trent the popes appointed a liturgical commission to produce books that would guide the liturgies throughout Catholicism. In the fifty years after Trent, Rome made major efforts to achieve this goal.

The first liturgical book published was a Roman breviary in 1568, which guided the daily prayers for priests. In 1570, a Roman Missal became the official sacramentary. To avoid the extremes of elaborate medieval Masses as well as the cold, dry, or private Masses, this Roman Missal guided the celebrant in a simplified and clear Mass with some excesses removed. In 1588, Pope Sixtus V formed the Congregation of Rites in Rome to deal with questions arising about the liturgy. Many of these came from the "New Worlds" being opened up since Columbus had crossed the Atlantic in 1492, which led not only to exploration, but also to evangelization. In 1596, a Roman Pontifical was published that guided bishops in their ceremonies and liturgies; in 1614, a Roman Ritual followed for the parish priest. "Rubricism" was coming into its own.

These collections led to a centralized and uniform Mass while clarifying what the Eucharist and Mass were for Catholics. It took place in the context of the many questions raised by the Protestants and the many ways in which they were celebrating Mass, which various Protestants called the Eucharist or, more commonly, the Lord's Supper. While mandatory, the 1570 Roman Missal allowed for the continuation of other rites that were over 200 years old, such as the Ambrosian rite in Milan and the Mozarabic rite in parts of Spain, as long as the diversity did not change the theology of the Eucharist and priesthood. These Catholic reformations did not end the private Masses, which left the problem of the overlooked communal aspect of the Mass unresolved in most places. People still watched rather than participated actively in the Mass. Although the Council of Trent encouraged receiving Communion, few Catholics did. But it was certainly hard now to misunderstand that the Eucharist was truly Jesus.

The Mass remained in Latin, although several times the delegates at Trent discussed the use of vernacular languages and saw its value. This became a thorny issue since the Protestants had quickly moved their liturgies into the dialects of their congregations. Some bishops and theologians at Trent suggested that Mass *could* be in the vernacular, but certainly that the sermon *should* be in the people's language. Trent did not agree with the Protestant idea that the liturgy must be in the vernacular. Bishops at the council emphasized that Latin provided a universal language that could unite all Catholics (even though few in the pews knew Latin) and provide a standard and fixed theological vocabulary. Vernacular languages might slip into heresy, they argued, because words in different languages held nuances, and these nuances might lead to different people thinking they believed the same thing when they did not. But Trent did say that bishops and priests should use the vernacular when explaining the sacraments and instructing the congregation in how they should live according to God's commandments. The council also ordered bishops to have the council's teachings on the sacraments translated into the vernacular. Trent may not have gone far enough for some, but it clarified many questions about the Mass.

The Early Modern Church: A Paradox

FOR SEVERAL CENTURIES AFTER TRENT, two developments in the liturgy seemed to contradict each other. On the one hand, the rules of liturgy were followed so closely and with so little diversity that this period can be seen as one of "rubricism." This means that priests and bishops followed the rules written in red in the sacramentaries (the rubrics) so closely and precisely that Mass felt like a reading of the letter of the law. But, at the same time, triumphalism marked this period, with extravagant art, architecture, and music adorning the liturgy and the church buildings. We should look at each development in turn.

Rubricism developed, in part, in reaction to the variety of Protestant beliefs and rites that challenged Catholicism and the Mass. While Protestants focused on the priesthood of all believers, the bishops at Trent emphasized the ordained priesthood, the Church's authority, and the uniformity of the liturgy. As a result, the priest at the altar became the focal point of the Mass. While understandable, at the same time this further distanced the people and discouraged their active participation. The system of private Masses continued, as well. In the city of Barcelona alone, requests for private Masses increased eight times in the sixteenth and seventeenth centuries. Mass remained in Latin and, after 1661, the Church even prohibited vernacular translations in missals for the people to use. Indeed, approved vernacular missals did not appear until 1897 in Europe and 1927 in the United States. Mass did not fall out of favor, however. Church authorities after Trent tried to focus the faithful toward the parish Mass and away from some of the medieval festivals that tended toward superstition. Because more people were attending Mass, parishes often had two Masses on Sundays. Also during these early modern centuries, the number of those receiving Holy Communion increased, with some Catholics confessing their sins and receiving the Eucharist four times a year or even monthly, though very rarely receiving from the chal-

ice. The Liturgy of the Eucharist remained the high
point of the Mass and one that the faithful were
directed to worship. Bells rang three times to call their
attention to the altar: at the offertory, the elevation,
and when the priest received Holy Communion.

If rubricism is one end of the story of the early
modern Mass, then triumphalism is the other. While
more frequent parish Masses could be rather sterile due
to liturgical rubricism with little congregational participation, the physical setting of Masses in major churches across Europe could be quite ornate. The word
"baroque" is usually associated with this triumphalism—referring in the least charitable sense to Catholicism's "triumph" over Protestantism. The style of
baroque art, architecture, and music is often described
with words like massive, colossal, awe-inspiring, dramatic, and full of the play of light with shadow.

The baroque style contrasted sharply with
Protestant churches, which were typically very plain,
spare, and austere. In addition, the altar had taken a less
central spot in Protestant churches, since some denominations celebrated a Lord's Supper only once a month.
The pulpit, used to preach the Word of God, was made
more central, and in Calvinist churches it often stood
right in the center of a round building. Starting in
Rome, some Catholic baroque architects placed the
altar in the central position, raised it up, and lit it with a
large dome overhead. In fact, when early modern
Catholics entered one of these churches, their eyes
were drawn not to the altar but to the tabernacle just
above it, which emphasized the Blessed Sacrament.

Other elements of the baroque style emphasized Catholic theology over Protestant ideas. Apart from the centrality of the Eucharist and the lasting Real Presence, painters and sculptors portrayed miracles of saints, purgatory, the sacraments, and the life of Mary, the Mother of God. The Jesuits' church in Rome, the Gesù, was sometimes called a "theater of salvation." Indeed, baroque churches are very dramatic. Instead of the medieval carnival in the town square and the Gothic cathedral's side altars, baroque artists and architects made the church the center of the town and the altar the center of the church.

Baroque music was used to create unified settings for the entire Mass and not just a few parts. During this period, musicians abandoned secular melodies and instruments for organs and a complex style of music called polyphony. This was more ornate than plainsong and most Gregorian chants from the Middle Ages. Baroque music was so operatic that it threatened to overwhelm the Mass and distract from the sacrament the priest was celebrating. After Trent, baroque music yielded to classical and then romantic musical styles, with Masses written by important composers such as Mozart, Haydn, Beethoven, and Schubert, each of them making Mass more theatrical.

As with many things, well-intentioned people went too far with very good ideas. In the largest cathedrals and cities, Mass was becoming a concert or symphony; although the more elaborate the music, the more lay people were involved as singers, these tended to be professionals and not the parishioners in the pews. Because

Mass was becoming too fancy, in a sense, and more performance than participation, some reformers raised their voices.

In Europe in the middle of the eighteenth century, for instance, lay people, priests, and bishops called for increased participation and understanding for the faithful. Some priests followed the letter of the rubrics by reading the Gospel in Latin, but then added a vernacular paraphrase of their own afterward. The most vocal reformers wanted the entire Mass to be translated into the vernacular, but that had to wait more than two centuries, until after Vatican II. Other priests did not simply whisper the words of the consecration, but said them loudly and slowly, while some parishes abandoned the simultaneous private Masses at side altars where they still existed in older church buildings. It is clear, then, that during this early modern period, the Mass was being pulled in two directions, leaving to the modern age the task of reconciling the two directions by avoiding their excesses and employing their good sides.

The Modern Church: Active Participation of the Faithful

FOR MOST CATHOLICS, LITURGICAL CHANGE in the modern Church means Vatican II. While this latest council, which met from 1962 to 1965, led to massive changes in the Mass, those changes had been developing since the late seventeenth century. These developments were known as the liturgical movement by the early twentieth century and eventually produced the Mass we celebrate today. Intense study began largely in France in the nineteenth century, centered around Dom Prosper Guéranger at the Benedictine monastery of Solesmes and spreading to Germany and Belgium. Soon, several academic and popular meetings, journals, and study centers of liturgical practice designed to help pastors and make parishioners more active in the Mass appeared in both Europe and North America. One person who read Guéranger's work was Cardinal Giuseppe Sarto, the archbishop of Venice who was later elected Pope Pius X (1903–1914).

A key phrase for the liturgical movement is "active participation of the faithful." Pius X was particularly interested in enlivening the liturgy and increasing the role and understanding of the person in the pew. With his document *Tra le sollecitudini* in 1903, Pius X encouraged the rediscovery of Gregorian chant, congregational singing, and the active participation of the faithful, including frequent and even daily reception of Holy Communion. In 1905, Pius X said that a Catholic who wanted to receive Communion could not be in mortal sin and had to desire to do God's will, but Communion did not have to be the first thing a person ate or drank, nor did the Catholic have to go to confession immediately before receiving. In 1910, he dropped the age for First Communion to the age of reason, which in practice usually became about seven years old. He believed a child of seven could tell the difference between regular bread and Eucharistic bread. These changes caused both adults and children to learn more about the Mass, and particularly the Church's teaching on the Eucharist.

In the 1920s and 1930s in Europe, "dialogue Masses" grew more popular and increased lay participation. The congregation joined the priest celebrating Mass in saying the *Gloria, Credo, Sanctus,* and *Agnus Dei,* as well as responding to phrases such as *"Dominus vobiscum,"* all of which remained in Latin, at least officially. More and more, Catholics were not just attending Mass, but celebrating the liturgy with the priest who was presiding. Scholars were writing histories of the Mass and sacred music; lay people were gathering to discuss the liturgy; and publishers produced small, inexpensive, and jargon-free explanations of Catholic rites and beliefs, especially as they concerned the Mass. The liturgical movement was crossing the Atlantic, too. In the United States, starting in 1926, Virgil Michel at St. John's Abbey in Collegeville, Minnesota, began a journal, set up a publishing house named Liturgical Press, and held annual meetings on the liturgy.

In the years between World War II and Vatican II, liturgical renewal blossomed. In 1947, Pope Pius XII (1939–1958) established a liturgical commission within the Vatican's Congregation of Rites, which was the first major step in the organized revision of the Mass. That same year, the papal document *Mediator Dei* continued Pius X's initiatives and gave approval to the liturgical movement as a sign of the Spirit at work. Pius XII allowed some vernacular rites, commissioned a new translation of the Psalms, and made it easier to receive Holy Communion by easing the fasting regulations to only a three-hour fast instead of from midnight. Pius XII also approved bilingual Masses for Europe, which allowed priests to use Latin and either French or German. In 1951, the Easter Vigil liturgy was restored to its original place on Saturday night, and four years later the various Holy Week liturgies were restored and revived. Pius XII approved vernacular hymns in 1953. By the late 1950s, Mass-goers would hear the epistle and Gospel first read in Latin, but then in their vernacular languages. By 1958, lay men (but not women) were permitted to read Scripture at Mass in the vernacular.

Vatican II and its key document on the liturgy, *Sacrosanctum Concilium,* energized the active participation of the faithful and stressed that people in the congregation must know and understand what is happening at the altar. The document spelled out the theology supporting the full, conscious, and active participation of the faithful. Soon after the council, the sanctuary was rearranged and Holy Communion given under both species. It wasn't long before altar rails disappeared, altars were turned so the priest faced the people, and congregants could receive Holy Communion in their hands, as the earliest Christians had done.

The changes flowed quickly. In 1964, pastors were reminded that they must preach every Sunday and on holy days of obligation. Later that year, the vernacular was approved for the opening greeting, readings, hymns, prayers of the faithful, and the Our Father. In 1967, the missal and Eucharistic prayers were revised, and a lectionary with a wider selection of readings was introduced. Two years later, the rites for Marriage, infant Baptism, and funerals were updated, followed in the early 1970s by new rites for Confirmation and the Rite of Christian Initiation of Adults. In 1969, Pope Paul VI (1963–1978) promulgated a new *General Instruction* for celebrating sacraments. In 1971, the vernacular Mass was finally approved, although in some places it had already been celebrated for several years. Many people experienced Vatican II's changes when they went to Mass or attended marriages, Baptisms, and funerals in the late 1960s and early 1970s.

Since Vatican II, of course, liturgical changes have sometimes caused controversy. Some who clung to the majesty and mystery of the "old" Mass and others who quickly embraced (and sometimes ran beyond) the reforms were often at odds with one another. Some, for example, point out that Vatican II did not specify the use of vernacular liturgies. *Sacrosanctum Concilium,* in fact, had said that Latin should be preserved, but also left it up to local bishops to decide if vernacular was the better way to go for their people. Within a short time, almost every bishops' conference in the world had petitioned Rome for permission to celebrate a vernacular liturgy. Between extremes lies a majority who have embraced and benefited from the more understandable rites, the greater range of Scripture, and the emphasis on the Eucharist—all in a language that is their own. Of course, there will always be some Catholics who like liturgical dance and altar girls while others can't stand the ideas. It is important to remember that the reforms are ongoing and that Mass continues to evolve in its forms, although the essentials can never be compromised. Where this will lead is, as always, up to the Holy Spirit. But it is worth remembering that a major source of Catholic unity should and must be the celebration of the Eucharist at Mass.

Chapter 6

THE SACRAMENTS

How did the seven sacraments come to be?

BEFORE BEGINNING AN EXPLORATION of how the Church got her seven sacraments, I want to stress that the idea of "development" applies more in this area of Church history than in any of the other areas treated in this book. Historians and theologians will search in vain through the first millennium of Christianity for a codification of the seven sacraments per se, but that does not mean that each of the seven sacraments was not present in its essentials from the earliest moments of the Church's life. They were not invented later, but how they were celebrated did evolve over time. For about a thousand years, ideas about the sacraments had a degree of flexibility, which came to be more standardized and fixed by the scholastic theologians of the Middle Ages. It took many more centuries for the theology and practice of these seven sacraments to develop into the form that we recognize today.

The Early Church: A Focus on Baptism

INITIATION—THAT IS, HOW TO BECOME a Christian—dominated the sacraments in the Church's first few centuries, which makes sense since the Church was being born. The first Church communities put Baptism (with a hint of Confirmation) and Eucharist together as what we call sacraments of initiation. A reminder of these roots and the combination of the sacraments of initiation is seen at today's Easter Vigil, when adults are baptized, receive the Eucharist, and can be confirmed by the presiding priest even if a bishop is not present.

Much of what we know about early baptisms comes from two sources: the *Apostolic Tradition* of the Roman

Hippolytus (ca. 225) and the *Didache*. The latter, an instruction manual for Christian initiation and life, may be one of the earliest Church documents, dating to the Holy Land just a few decades after Jesus. The baptisms they describe, with an anointing we might be tempted to identify as a separate sacrament of Confirmation, typically came after two or three years of preparation and scrutiny, with the final period occurring naturally during Lent. During this process—as is done in today's Church—the candidates would study the Creed and prayers, then at a certain point be tested so that at their baptisms they could declare their faith and its practices for themselves. Just like today's catechumens, potential Christians could attend the Liturgy of the Word, but not the Eucharist. At the Easter Vigil, dressed in white after their baptisms, they would bring up the offertory gifts and receive the Eucharist for the first time. We should note, however, that an intellectual understanding of Christianity was important, but the preparation time focused more on making sure the catechumens learned the Christian way of life: how to follow Jesus and live as he lived.

Early baptisms would be familiar to us: there was a renunciation of evil and a profession of faith. The Sign of the Cross would be made on the forehead, followed by an exchange of peace and a laying on of hands. The new Christian was usually naked and immersed entirely in water three times—once for each person of the Trinity, with an anointing with oil (on the head, hands, or even feet) after the immersions. The immersions represented cleansing as well as the candidate's death to sin and rebirth to new life in the risen Jesus. The catechumen had to be immersed by someone else. The water was supposed to be cold and running naturally, as in a river or stream, but large baths came to be used, surely for practical purposes. For about 200 years after Jesus, mostly adults were baptized, although infant Baptism, particularly of the children of baptized adults, was practiced at least from the second century. Infant Baptism began to appear more frequently by the early third century, with parents answering the questions about the faith for their children, as godparents do today. By the fifth or sixth century, infant Baptism with godparents seems to have been fairly common, except for adult converts. Tertullian, a North African theologian writing in Latin in the late second and early third century, identified four effects of initiation: remission of sins, deliverance from death, regeneration, and the bestowal of the Holy Spirit. By the early third century, it appears that Christian theologians believed the bestowal of the Holy Spirit was effected not by the waters of Baptism, but by the anointing with oil, which we can see as a forerunner of Confirmation as a distinct sacrament.

Penance occurred at first just once in a person's lifetime—which is why potential Christian converts might put Baptism off until very late in life—and it was a public, communal event that mirrored the catechumenate. The emphasis was originally disciplinary: it was a way of separating the sinner physically from the faith community until he or she could be "reconciled" back. A model might have been Peter, who denied Christ, who felt sorrow and repentance, and who was then reconciled with Jesus. Major sins were idolatry, murder, and adultery or incest. John Cassian, a Church Father and monk writing in the early 400s, identified eight other sins: gluttony, fornication, greed, anger, despair, laziness, vanity, and pride.

The issue of apostasy was especially troublesome during the Roman persecutions of Christians, and it shaped Penance. In many cases, Christians who had not really renounced Christ but had spared their lives by bribing Roman officials or buying phony certificates saying that they had sacrificed to the pagan gods were reconciled after several weeks of public penance. This was especially true if someone who had actually suffered for the faith sponsored their readmission. But those who had indeed sacrificed to the gods were reconciled only after long periods of penitence, which could last up to a dozen years, although some believed apostasy was unforgivable. Penitents could hear the Word from the back of the church and over time work their way up to the front of the congregation. Like catechumens, they could not receive the Eucharist. After a period of prayer, penitence, good works, and tithing, they were returned to the community during Holy Week, typically on Holy Thursday, with the bishop or priest laying hands and offering a prayer of forgiveness.

We find other sacraments developing in the early Church, too. Anointing of the Sick was connected to healing, as it had been for Jesus and the apostles. Orders, or ordinations, denoted a certain class or group of people with particular duties. In his *Apostolic Tradition,* Hippolytus tells us that to be a bishop, priest, or deacon, an ordination had to take place. This was comprised of the laying on of hands to call down the Holy Spirit, at least, and often an anointing, too. The community's leaders then appointed readers, acolytes, and other ministers, but these received a prayer and blessing, not the laying on of hands. Certain days came to be customary for ordinations: bishops on Sundays, for example, and priests and deacons on Saturday evenings.

The order of deacons was especially integral to the early Church. Deacons were married ministers who led prayers and helped at the altar, baptized, and probably preached. They were closely connected with their bishops and played a special role in teaching catechumens and in helping widows, orphans, and the poor. By the end of this first period of Church history, however, their functions were already being greatly restricted. Their golden age had ended to await the renewal of the permanent diaconate with Vatican II.

Marriage in the early Church, meanwhile, usually followed society's norms: a priest or blessing was not required, but there had to be mutual and free consent given by bride and groom with witnesses present. One of the fathers typically presided, at home, and oversaw the dowry, ring exchange, and the Roman custom of clasping right hands. However, Christians could not divorce, remarry, or marry non-Christians.

The First Millennium Church: Gradual Developments

AS THE CHURCH MOVED FROM THE persecutions of the Roman Empire to become the new glue of Western society, her sacraments developed gradually. During this period, the Church was not at her most creative, but she did advance sacramental theology and practice, leaving a legacy for the medieval explosion of ideas and rites.

Adult Baptism remained common, especially in central Europe, Britain, and Ireland, as missionary bishops, abbots, and monks spread the faith northward from the Mediterranean basin. But infant Baptism was also very common for the children of those adults, with godparents taking the role of answering questions and sponsoring the children. Infants were also baptized soon after their births because of the high rates of infant mortality. Because of the increase in infant Baptism, a change developed in the ritual, with water being poured over the child's head in place of the full body immersion. Gradually, sprinkling came to replace full immersion even for adults.

Confirmation was moved away from Baptism in the last centuries of the first millennium before being definitively separated from Baptism in the eleventh century. Catechumens would be baptized but not confirmed at the same time. We find the word "confirmation" used separately in Gaul (modern France) starting in the fifth century. Bishops frequently traveled throughout their dioceses, almost like circuit court judges in the nineteenth-century United States. When they visited a particular region, the bishops would confirm all those new Christians who had been baptized since their last visits, regardless of age.

Penance enjoyed some lively growth in Ireland and Wales, where monks played a large role in lay spirituality. Penance moved away from its roots as a public, communal, and unrepeatable event to become private, individual, and repeatable. This development grew partly from a tradition of spiritual direction, where Christians would visit a monk for advice. This mirrored the way monks and nuns sought direction from their abbots and abbesses. Irish missionary monks took this practice with them when they traveled to Gaul, Spain, England, and Italy to evangelize the non-Christians in those regions.

A handbook system developed, with sins written in one column on a page and the corresponding penance on the other. Some of these sound remarkably modern and logically counsel a person to do the opposite of the sin. If sinners are angry, they should be patient; if they are greedy, they should give freely; if they are gluttonous, they should fast. Often, the penitent was sent away to perform the penance and had to return for absolution. The intent was to help penitents change their ways, especially during Lent, through private confession of their sins and very specific, even practical, penance that had to be done before the penitents received absolution. Penance continued to be linked with the Anointing of the Sick when a person was near death. We find in Spain and Gaul references to blessings of oil that mention the healing action of the Holy Spirit and describe Christ as a great physician, which is an idea inherited from the Church's first few centuries.

Ordinations became more specific and elaborate. A priest being ordained a bishop received a pallium (a circle of cloth around the neck to symbolize his jurisdiction). A book of the Gospels was placed over his head to show the Church's protection, and he sat on an epis-copal throne to show his teaching authority. He was also anointed and invested with a crosier, a miter, and a ring. A new priest received a chalice, paten, bread, and wine; the new deacon was presented with a book of the Gospels. By this time, deacons were almost exclu-sively "transitional" in preparation for priesthood. A sys-tem of minor orders developed to go with the major ones of bishop, priest, and deacon. These minor orders did not entail ordination, but were conveyed with the tool of the order's task: porter (key), lector (lectionary), exorcist (rite for exorcisms), acolyte (candle and cruet), and subdeacon (chalice, paten, cruets, basin, and towel).

Marriage, meanwhile, seemed to continue the early Church's lack of specificity and procedures, although a blessing by a priest (as opposed to the bride's father) was preferred to make the point that it was God who united the couple. In Spain, this point was made by the priest giving the bride away. The blessing could take place at the door of the church or in the couple's house—or bedroom—at the time of the engagement or wedding.

Finally, an important debate on the Eucharist took place during the Carolingian Renaissance under the Emperor Charlemagne (768–814), when three monks treated the Real Presence of the Eucharist. Paschasius Radbertus (790–865) wrote *On the Body and Blood of the Lord,* which is the first systematic doctrinal treatise on the Eucharist. He placed great emphasis on Christ's physical presence in the Eucharist, saying that it is the same actual, physical body that hung on the cross. Rhabanus Maurus (784–856) reacted strongly against this position and emphasized the spiritual aspects of the Eucharist so much that he said the Real Presence existed only in the mind of the believer. Ratramnus (d. 868) tried to argue a middle way by stating that the Eucharist was the Real Presence of Christ's spiritual body, not the same actual physical body from the cross—a position adopted by many Protestants 700 years later. It is clear, then, that this period of alleged "dark ages" was no wasteland of sacramental theology.

The Medieval Church: Consolidation and Clarity

THE RISE OF SCHOLASTIC THEOLOGY in the Middle Ages led the Church to organize and codify canon law, liturgy, systematic theology, and the sacraments. In Paris, the theology professor Peter Lombard (ca. 1100–1160) synthesized centuries of speculation, debate, and practice concerning sacramental theology to fix the number of sacraments at seven and to explain how they worked. The Middle Ages, then, was a period of great organization and clarity for the Church's sacraments, although Baptism and Confirmation largely continued to operate as they had by the end of the first millennium.

Building on centuries of speculation and teaching about the Eucharist, in 1215 the Fourth Lateran Council used the word "transubstantiation" to describe how the bread and wine at Mass became the Real Presence of the body and blood of Jesus Christ, though it appears to human eyes that bread and wine remain. This was not a new teaching, but a clearer way of explaining what the Church had always believed about Christ's presence in the Eucharist. Lateran IV said Christians should confess their sins and receive the Eucharist once a year, which ended up being referred to as the "Easter duty." The "age of discretion" at which Christians received their First Communion was typically seven to twelve years old.

The individual reception of Penance continued to develop from the first millennium, although public demonstrations of penance were common in the Middle Ages. During Holy Week processions in particular, penitents (hooded for anonymity) would march through town beating or flailing themselves for their sins. Handbooks for private confessions sometimes took a question-and-answer format that the priest could use to guide the penitent through an examination of conscience. Once the sins were identified, the corresponding penance could be assigned. As before, the penitent then left, performed the penitential action, and returned for absolution from the confessor. A formula began to develop for the entire process, and the Latin phrase *"Ego te absolvo..."* ("I absolve you...") was commonly used by the thirteenth century. Unfortunately, this handbook approach sometimes became a bit mechanical. In addition, some penitents were permitted to pay for the absolution in place of performing the penitential act. This "tariff" approach was clearly open to abuse and was a formula for disaster, as the Protestant reformers pointed out within a few centuries.

The Church continued to organize itself, especially from about 500 to 1200. After the Roman Empire fell, the papacy stepped in to unite Europe. During this time the sacrament of Orders became increasingly important. The Church needed an elite leadership that was clearly marked off in order to safeguard the integrity of the sacraments. The minor orders (acolyte, lector, etc.) were subsumed into the steps achieved on the way to priesthood. By the late twelfth century, the subdiaconate was raised to the level of a major order. A more elaborate ritual developed for a man to become a subdeacon, but it still did not include laying on of hands.

Anointing of the Sick and Marriage benefited from this clarity with respect to the Church's authority and her exclusive ability to confer sacramentality. Anointing was to take place in the context of Mass or at least a prayer service, often connected with the Eucharist and/or Penance. After a laying on of hands, oil was applied, sometimes with a brush, to the face or head, hands, ears, eyes, mouth, nostrils, and chest. A book of the Scriptures was often held over the sick person's head as well, with a passage read from James 5:13–16. This text speaks of how the earliest Christians prayed with each other, were prayed over and anointed by their elders, confessed their sins, and were forgiven.

Marriage continued its slow development as a sacrament with as much attention paid to its theology and ritual as to that of other sacraments. Most significantly, marriage was fully recognized as a sacrament in the Middle Ages. The wedding ceremony was moved to the church, albeit still only at the door and not the altar, at least for the commoners (99 percent of the people). Aristocrats or royalty were permitted to stand before the altar. Because of the frequent concern that the woman was being forced into marriage instead of freely consenting, the wedding had to be public and not private—or "secret" or "clandestine," as the sources sometimes call it. The ceremony consisted of the mutual exchange of consent by bride and groom, an instruction by the priest, the bestowal of dowry and ring (for the woman, but rarely the man), and a blessing that, like the rest of the ceremony, was in Latin except for the consent and instruction. All of these rituals still largely mirrored the civil practices for legal reasons, but now they were imbued with religious significance and, indeed, sacramentality without a doubt.

Church councils paid special attention to the sacrament of Marriage. Lateran I (1123) and Lateran II (1139) said that when members of the same family married, they were guilty of incest in the eyes of both Church and civil law. Since medieval Europe was not a very mobile society, however, this led to problems. Most of the population lived in the countryside, where just a few extended families comprised isolated villages separated by fair distances. Christians had to be permitted to marry within a reasonable degree of blood relation, known as consanguinity, or they could not marry and have families at all, practically speaking. How close was too close? In 1215 Lateran IV clarified the matter: four degrees of separation must be maintained, which in effect meant that a Christian could not marry anyone closer than a second cousin. More than any other sacrament during the Middle Ages, Marriage had come into its own.

The Reformation Church:
Affirming Seven Sacraments

IN RETROSPECT, IT WAS A VERY GOOD thing indeed that the medieval Church had consolidated her thinking on the sacraments, codified their number at seven, and clarified precisely what the sacraments meant and did. This enabled the Church to meet the difficulties of the Reformation period, when a variety of Protestant reformers challenged the number and meaning of Catholic sacraments from several angles.

Martin Luther (1483–1546), Jean Calvin (1509–1564), and the other Protestant reformers who branched off from them criticized and challenged the very heart of the sacramental system. Their critiques questioned the Church's teachings on essential issues: sinfulness, redemption, and how to get to heaven. To some extent Luther made reasonable criticisms against human excesses—like people snatching up indulgences to pay for the time they would otherwise have to spend in purgatory or to gain the good done by certain penances without actually doing them. But Luther and others went beyond criticizing the abuse of the indulgence system to say that the very system itself, tied up as it was with the idea that Christians can participate via good works in their salvation, was flawed.

Luther, and Calvin even more so, accentuated God's role in salvation and humanity's sinfulness. While Luther believed that Catholics overemphasized the human dimension and the idea that human actions have merit toward salvation, Calvin knocked humans entirely out of the equation. Calvin maintained that God and God alone predestined human beings for heaven or hell, and an individual person could do nothing to change that fate. This notion attacked the Catholic sacramental system at its core because sacraments are agents of grace that help Catholics become holy, turn away from sin, grow closer to God, and work with Jesus to attain eternal salvation. If, as Luther and Calvin said, humans are justified by faith alone, then what role do the sacraments play? And if Christians don't need sacraments, what does that mean about the need for priests and their role as mediators, especially given the Protestant principle of the priesthood of all believers?

Protestants generally reduced the number of sacraments to two or three (Baptism, Penance, and Eucharist), with varying definitions. Concerning the Eucharist, Luther asserted that, while Jesus is really present, transubstantiation was wrong. Instead, he said that the bread and wine remain along with Jesus' body and blood, which he called "consubstantiation." Calvin and his followers kept Baptism and Eucharist, but said Jesus was only symbolically present in bread and wine that never changed at all. For most Protestants, the Mass was not the Catholic sacrifice but only a memorial, which they increasingly called the Lord's Supper. Other Protestants asserted that humans were not born with Original Sin that had to be washed away by Baptism, but that in sinning Adam and Eve had set a bad example that did not subsequently taint all of humanity. Baptism therefore was a person's symbolic acceptance of Jesus as his or her Savior or an initiation into the community of believers. So it should be undertaken only by adults making a conscious choice, not by infants with godparents speaking for them.

How did Catholicism respond? After a great deal of internal debate and delay, the Council of Trent met in three phases (1545–1547, 1551–1552, 1562–1563). Among its many explanations, Trent built on medieval theology to affirm that there were indeed seven sacraments and to describe their natures and purposes. Because Luther and the others had challenged core principles, the council clarified Church teaching on Original Sin and justification, then explained how the sacraments fit into that theology. Trent reached back to Lateran IV (1215) to explain transubstantiation again as the Real Presence of Jesus and to assert that the Eucharist was a sacrament. It also explained what Baptism, Confirmation, Penance, Anointing, Orders, and Marriage were and why they were sacraments, often to counter Protestant ideas. Penance, for instance, was out of favor with certain Protestants who did not believe that a priest was needed as mediator. They thought that a person could reconcile with God on his or her own or participate in a group exercise of confession and reconciliation. Trent, in response, reasserted the role of priest and penitent as well as what is called auricular confession: one person at a time confessing his or her specific sins aloud to a priest in a private celebration of the sacrament.

Trent's reforms reinvigorated the sacraments, starting with the sacraments of initiation. Infant Baptism remained, the role of the godparents was emphasized and proper instruction was provided for them. The council authorized a catechism, which came out in 1566, to reaffirm Catholic teachings in the aftermath of the Protestant Reformation. This catechism supposed that Christians who had been baptized as infants would be confirmed between the ages of seven and twelve when the bishop was available. Christians still received the Eucharist infrequently, but sometimes more often than simply making their Easter duty. Catholics may have received Communion four times a year, which translates into once each season, and some may have received once a month. Confirmations rebounded from a certain decline in the Middle Ages, too.

Penance manuals similar to their early medieval ancestors began to appear after Trent to guide both confessor and penitent. These books emphasized the continued spiritual growth of the penitent rather than Penance as a quick opportunity to review and dispense with a laundry list of sins. The idea of Marriage as a sacrament became a greater part of marriage preparation. Trent reasserted strongly the marriage legislation of the medieval Lateran councils and put the parish priest in charge of making sure everything was done properly.

Partly because of the Protestant discussions of the priesthood of all believers, the sacrament of Orders—especially priesthood—was stressed very much, which widened the gap between clergy and laity. But a positive development from Trent's affirmation of how sacraments are celebrated produced a slow-but-steady improvement, over a century or two, of training for priests. Trent, in essence, invented seminaries in the way we think of them today, which led to priests who were more theologically literate. Trent also emphasized the pastoral role of the bishop, which in turn led to increased respect for the Church's shepherds and to new bishops who were better qualified and more suitable for their roles because of their pastoral, not political, skills.

The Early Modern Church: Implementing Trent

In the centuries after Trent, no striking developments occurred in any particular sacrament, except for Penance. During these centuries, the Church settled down after the Protestant Reformation and the Council of Trent. It began to implement the seven sacraments by explaining them to the faithful and encouraging lay people to celebrate the sacraments with faith and understanding. Indeed, Trent's catechism made clear that proper catechesis must precede the first celebration of each sacrament.

In the years after Trent, one noticeable change began to appear in the celebration of sacraments: the more common appearance of the confessional box for Penance in churches. It was generally set off for privacy but was open: the priest and penitent could be seen to prevent any opportunity for impropriety. It was assumed the confessor knew the penitent and could guide him or her appropriately, according to the person's unique disposition and spiritual journey. Early in the seventeenth century, new practice arose: grills began to be installed so the priest and penitent could not see each other, which gave anonymity to the penitent. By this time, Penance had long lost its public dimensions, which indeed had not been essential for nearly a millennium, except for the non-sacramental penitential processions of the Middle Ages. Penance became not only private, but anonymous.

Absolution was still not always given as part of the penitent's confession. Something of a theological debate developed. Led by Jesuit theologians and confessors, "probabilists" offered absolution at the time of confession if it was probable that a penitent was truly contrite. (Probabilists would give Communion based on the same principle.) "Rigorists" opposed the probabilists and wanted Catholics to abstain from the sacraments unless they were positive that they were pure and prepared in both their actions and their wills. Rigorists, hearkening back to earlier chapters in Church history, wanted confessors to assign a penance that would have to be performed before the penitent returned for absolution. This action, according to the rigorists, would prove the penitent's contrition and demonstrate that the person truly merited absolution.

Meanwhile, Mass remained the focus of parish life and was celebrated with vigor in Europe's large cities and small villages. But as the Church spread to the "New World," Catholicism in Britain's American colonies was a minority religion in an Anglican setting. Although Catholicism was certainly not outlawed in the way Christianity had been during its early life in the Roman Empire, the faith was again relegated to second-class status, at least, and had to deal with some harsh attitudes. In fact, in 1704, the British Anglican governor of the Maryland colony referred to Catholic Masses as "gaudy shows." Most Catholics celebrated Mass in small groups in private chapels in homes, or simply in their dining or living room.

Colonial American Catholics probably received Communion fairly regularly, perhaps as much as once a month, but more commonly three to four times per year. Mass was not always available every Sunday at a convenient location, however, since there were few priests, especially before the American Revolution.

Early in the nineteenth century, Penance was celebrated by most people about once a year, with once a month for those few Catholics who were especially fervent and had access to a priest with some regularity. Communion and Penance were therefore more common in the few cities than in the many small villages—a circumstance true for both Europe and the New World.

Among the other sacraments, Anointing of the Sick had, over the course of the Middle Ages and Reformation, come to be celebrated most commonly on a person's deathbed. This gave it the popular names "extreme unction" (typically garbled as something like "extramunction") or "last rites." The rite involved was shortened—understandably, since time was often an issue with a dying person—and came to be known as *Viaticum*. The rite included the reception of Communion and confession with absolution, if that were possible given the physical state of the dying person.

Marriage during this period sometimes became, at least for the elites, somewhat more legalistic and supervised, since inheritance issues were often involved. In colonial America and after the American Revolution, mixed marriages between Catholics and non-Catholics were uncommon, but they did occur. They were perhaps more frequent in America than in Europe, where the memory of the Protestant-Catholic split remained and was more socially and politically palpable. The marriage rite itself was now definitively moved to the altar, where the exchange of consent was always witnessed by a priest, with the family taking a secondary role. Local customs were permitted, however, and a common one was still the blessing of the couple's marriage bed.

The sacraments of initiation were continuing to solidify around certain ages. Infant Baptism, except for converts, of course, had been the norm for many centuries. Confirmation was still celebrated almost exclusively when the bishop made pastoral visits to the various regions of his diocese. Trent had mandated that diocesan bishops (also called "ordinaries") visit every region of their dioceses. While this meant that no individual age was made preferable for Confirmation, in practice young Catholics were confirmed between the ages of seven and twelve. First Communion was commonly received at age eleven or twelve, which put it after Confirmation and not before. Even during these early modern centuries, however, some theologians, bishops, and pastors thought First Communion should come before Confirmation, which demonstrates that sacramental theology continued to develop on the eve of modernity.

The Modern Church:
Before and After Vatican II

Vatican II's changes are very visible in the way we celebrate the sacraments. But certain movements to increase
the celebration and understanding of the sacraments
actually predated Vatican II and paved the way for even
more developments in the council's aftermath. Much has
changed in recent decades, but these changes were often
a return to prior means of celebrating sacraments.

Some readers may still recall Saturdays' long lines to
the confessional that predated the council, often as a
way of lamenting that no one goes to Confession anymore. One study showed, for example, that in 1963, 37
percent of American Catholics surveyed confessed once
a month, but by 1974 that figure had fallen to 17 percent. Those long lines date back to the middle of the
nineteenth century, when parish missions grew in popularity. Under the guidance of Redemptorist and Paulist
preachers especially, missions focused on a return to the
sacraments, especially to Communion via Penance.

In 1974, the rite was altered to emphasize dialogue
and instruction. The very language of the sacrament
changed from "Confession" and "Penance" to Reconciliation. Confessional boxes were reconfigured into
Reconciliation rooms that gave the penitent the option
of celebrating the sacrament face-to-face with the
priest or in anonymity. The rite includes an examination of conscience beforehand, which is sometimes part
of a communal service, then private confession of sins,
instruction, an assignment of penance—which, as with

its origins, can be tied into making amends with a person offended, including God of course—a statement of contrition, and absolution at that time. Penitents are encouraged to think of this sacrament in terms of self-reflection, spiritual growth, and healing.

Healing is also emphasized in, to use its full name, the Rite of Anointing and Pastoral Care of the Sick and Dying. This sacrament has moved away from extreme unction, although Catholics and non-Catholics alike still incorrectly refer to the "last rites," especially in dramatic news reports about a Catholic's death. The emphasis is now on a sacrament that can be repeated, need not be administered at the point of death (or even danger of death), and that helps people of various ages who are sick physically and emotionally. Anointing with its renewed emphasis on healing has become a gift especially to those facing operations and chronic illnesses.

The sacrament of Orders was transformed in several ways. Pope Paul VI was especially interested in returning to early Church roots. First, the minor orders were deemphasized, and the subdiaconate was eliminated. Lay people took up some of these functions, especially as lectors and acolytes (and, most recently, with altar girls, too), which they had been doing in some places before Vatican II. Second, ordination rituals were simplified and brought in line with the Church's first traditions, often drawing on early documents like Hippolytus's *Apostolic Tradition* from early third-century Rome. The emphasis on bishop and priest as two parts of the priesthood returned: we talk now of episcopal ordination as the fullness of the priesthood.

Ordination for bishops, priests, and deacons share certain features: presentation of candidates, a public proclamation of the pope's appointment of a bishop or the bishop's acceptance of the candidates to be priests or deacons, a homily of instruction, prostration and litany of the saints, imposition of hands, a prayer of consecration, and a vesting. Ordination actually occurs with the imposition of hands and the consecratory prayer. The rite has some specific features, too. Bishops are anointed with chrism on their heads; are presented with a book of the Gospels, a ring, a miter, and a crosier; and are then seated on a chair or throne. Priests are anointed on their hands and presented with a chalice and paten since they can now celebrate the Eucharist. Deacons receive a book of the Gospels because they can now proclaim the Gospel. With the bishop's permission or when baptizing and witnessing marriages, they can also preach.

But the third and most important modern development in Orders was the renewal of the diaconate, with the ordination of permanent deacons who can be married. This broadened the diaconate beyond transitional deacons, who cannot be married and who are on their way to priesthood. The movement began in nineteenth-century Germany and took hold especially in Europe, South America, and the United States after World War II. Paul VI approved the permanent diaconate's restoration in 1967, and the next year the first permanent deacons were ordained in Germany and Cameroon. Americans followed in 1969. Nearly half of the world's permanent deacons are now serving in the United States.

The rate of receiving Communion rose after Vatican II, but that rate had been on the increase for over fifty years, dating back to several twentieth-century popes who encouraged the faithful to receive often. In one Portland, Oregon, parish, for instance, only 330 Communions were recorded for the entire year of 1919. Just four years later, there were 14,400 Communions—and this happened without an increase in the number of parishioners. Even today, while Mass attendance has declined, it appears that most people in the congregation receive the Eucharist.

Marriage has also come into its own, as it began to do in the Middle Ages, with a greater understanding among brides and grooms that they, and not the witnessing priest, celebrate the sacrament of Marriage by marrying each other. Couples participate more in the marriage ceremony by selecting their readings, but the rite itself retains much from earlier Church history: a welcome, the free giving of consent, holding right hands, an exchange of vows and rings (with the man now often wearing one, too), the nuptial blessing, and local customs. Vatican II also emphasized the family's sacred role as the domestic church, built on the sacrament of Marriage.

There have been, and continue to be, developments in the order and rites of the sacraments of initiation. Baptism remains for infants, but for the first time in Church history there is a rite of Baptism written specifically for infants, instead of merely shortening the formula for adults. This new rite focuses attention on the parents who bring their infant for Baptism and who, by doing so, accept the responsibility to raise their child in the Catholic faith. The Church also restored the Rite of Christian Initiation of Adults (RCIA) and a revised Confirmation rite (minus the infamous, but often gentle, slap to the face) in the early 1970s. RCIA especially returned the Church to her initiation roots in her first few centuries and follows the original sequence of the sacraments of initiation as, in order, Baptism, Confirmation, and Eucharist—typically during the Easter Vigil Mass. The age of Confirmation for children who were baptized as infants remains an issue today. In the United States, children may be confirmed any time between the ages of seven and fifteen, which sometimes leads to a break with the traditional sequence of Confirmation before Eucharist. Consider, for instance, all of those First Communions for second graders and Confirmations for teenagers that you may have attended. Sometimes, as a practical matter, Confirmation is held back so Catholic children in public schools will continue their religious education into their teenage years. In some places, First Communion and Confirmation are celebrated at the same Mass.

All of this rearranging and discussing is a reminder that the sacraments are not at issue, but their order of reception is. This is yet another example of the Church not changing her sacraments in their essentials at all, but continuing to work out the best way to use the seven sacraments given by Jesus over two millennia ago in our modern and changing world.

Chapter 7

SPIRITUALITY

What forms of spirituality developed?

The Early Church:
A Daily Code of Conduct

IN THE FIRST FEW CENTURIES AFTER JESUS, three major aspects of spirituality developed: the daily exercise of charity, a growing respect for asceticism, and the ultimate sacrifice of martyrdom. Over time, these spiritual exercises were joined by an organized set of feast days.

The Acts of the Apostles and the epistles in the New Testament demonstrate that the very first generations of Christian believers accentuated the daily living out of the virtues that Christ himself exhibited. The daily focus was probably tied into the fact that the first Christians believed Christ would return very quickly, so they felt they should be prepared for the end times. Early Christian spirituality, therefore, emphasized the gathering together of a community under the Holy Spirit waiting for Jesus.

As time passed and Jesus did not return, spirituality changed its focus from waiting for Jesus to return to preparing to meet Jesus at death. The most obvious preparation was to live by a moral code of conduct that marked believers as people of Christian (not Roman) purity, integrity, and service. Though we take living a moral life for granted, in fact, this first form of Christian spirituality set Christians apart from pagans who practiced idolatry, dabbled in magical rituals (prophecy and soothsaying), attended theatrical and gladiatorial spectacles, and lived by a sexual code that was incompatible with Jesus' teachings. As the first Christians put it, their goal was simple: to do the Lord's will.

So the first spirituality was very fundamental and focused on everyday challenges. This was no "Sunday faith," but a lived experience of religious commitment. Some letters dating from Rome about 95 to 125 show evidence of Christians fighting the secular and material pagan culture around them. Instead, they practiced chastity (having only one spouse), parental responsibility (by not abandoning their children), obedience, mercy, forgiveness, hospitality, friendship, almsgiving, repentance, fasting, humility, prayer, and Scripture study. They also practiced what came to be called the corporal works of mercy, such as visiting the sick and burying the dead—all the things Christians should do in order to work toward a continual conversion of their hearts to God.

Martyrs, on the other hand, were the first heroes or stand-out stars of Christianity, especially around the time of the worst of the Romans' periodic persecutions: under the emperors Nero in 64, Decius from 249–251, and Diocletian from 303–305. The most extreme form of spirituality, martyrdom was considered the highest spiritual victory and triumph over a Roman culture that treated Christians as traitors, atheists, and enemies. Christians had such fervor, even desire, for martyrdom, that in North Africa they greeted each other not with "Good morning," but "May you gain your crown." The anniversaries of martyrs' deaths were celebrated as their birthdays, since on that day they entered heaven's new life. A martyr's relics—which might be a cloth soaked in blood or a piece of clothing—were believed to have the power to cure and were held up in processions. A "cult" of martyrs emerged, and pilgrims would walk along Roman roads to visit their graves, a spiritual act that further set Christians apart from Romans. Pagans did not embrace death as a part of life and generally considered objects connected to death—especially corpses—as dangerous. When the body of Stephen, the first martyr, was found in Jerusalem in 415, the spirituality surrounding the cult of the martyr surged even though the age of martyrdom had passed once Constantine favored Christianity early in the fourth century.

Varying levels of ascetical practices stood between the daily spirituality of service and the extreme of martyrdom. Through these practices Christians would try to separate themselves from a sometimes hostile Roman culture throughout the Mediterranean world. The Christian, especially the ascetic, was something like a border figure: living in one world (without submitting to its baser elements) while preparing to live in the next world. That world could not be evil because God made it, and Jesus, through the Incarnation, lived in God's created universe. But that world had lost its way since the Fall, so the Christian was called to sanctify this world while getting ready for the next. Ascetics rejected the Roman world entirely by withdrawing from its cities into mountainside caves or deserts to live an extreme spirituality centered around both material and spiritual poverty. They lived alone or within a fair distance of other ascetics. They abstained from sexual intercourse, from meat and wine, and from owning property. They left their huts or caves to beg alms and often disciplined their bodies through self-flagellation or long fasts.

Sometimes they developed a negative view of creation, human nature, and the human body because of sin's effects, but they also became the Church's next heroes after the age of the martyrs had passed.

Finally, we can see spirituality cohering around feast days and seasons. Sunday was the first organized feast day because Jesus rose from the dead on the first day of the week. Weekly celebrations of this event followed logically and Sunday became known as the Lord's Day. It wasn't until 321, however, that Constantine made Sunday a holiday, which meant Christians could legally take the day off from work and celebrate Mass openly. Easter began to be celebrated on the Sunday after the Jewish Passover, but Christians in Asia Minor (and, later, Ireland) dated the feast differently, which threatened unity. The First Council of Nicaea in 325 decreed that Easter was to be celebrated around the first full moon after the spring equinox. Holy Week as a related cycle of feasts began in Jerusalem in the fourth century, after Constantine and his mother Helena built several shrines commemorating Jesus' life and passion. By the end of that century, Lent had developed into a period of forty fasting days, including the final preparation for catechumens.

In early Christianity the Easter events overshadowed Christmas, but it became natural to mark Jesus' beginnings, too. December 25 had been a Roman pagan holiday celebrating the winter solstice (the "shortest day of the year"—our December 21) and the birth of the invincible Sun-God. In 274, the Roman Emperor Aurelian made it an official holiday, but for the pagan and not the Christian God. Once Constantine favored

Christianity, it was easy to convert the celebration of the birthday of the pagan Sun-God to the birthday of the "Son-God" Jesus, since people were already disposed to mark this feast. Christians, of course, had been fooling the Roman pagans for centuries by secretly celebrating Christ's birth under the guise of marking the pagan feast.

The First Millennium Church: Seasons and Synthesis

CHRISTIAN SPIRITUALITY CONTINUED to develop through the organization of feast days and seasons. Simultaneously, a certain diversity in spiritual practices also appeared. It tried to Christianize elements of pagan religions in a way that drew new believers in Jesus toward Christian spirituality while permitting some familiar practices to continue.

Feast days are a good way to teach the faith and to direct spiritual practices. In 529, the Roman Emperor Justinian made December 25 an official Christian holy day and holiday. Christmas became a day for important events. In 598, Augustine of Canterbury is said to have baptized 10,000 people. Even if the number is exaggerated, as historians say, it still indicates that a mass Baptism took place on this day, of all days of the year. On December 25, 800, Pope Leo III crowned Charlemagne emperor in Rome.

Midnight Mass became a focus of spiritual devotion during this period, although we lack precise historic or New Testament evidence that Jesus was born at midnight. Justification for Midnight Mass came from a passage in Wisdom 18:14–15 that reads: "For while gentle silence enveloped all things, and night in its swift course was now half gone, your all-powerful word leaped from heaven, from the royal throne...." By the late fourth century, Midnight Mass appeared in Bethlehem. Midnight Mass moved to Rome in the fifth century: when popes recreated Bethlehem's manger scenes in Roman churches, it seemed logical to transfer the liturgical celebration, too. About the same time, representations of manger scenes from the Holy Land also appeared in the catacombs and churches in and around Rome. This path provides another example of spirituality moving from the people on the outskirts of Christianity to the Roman and papal center, which in turn helped legitimize and spread what the Church's central leadership saw as a devotion worth sharing.

Liturgical seasons soon followed to guide the Christians' spiritual preparations for major feasts. Ash Wednesday as the start of Lent appeared in the seventh century. Advent, with roots in Gaul and Spain dating back to the 300s, was fixed by a Church council in 567. Pope Gregory the Great (590–606) promoted this as a season of preparation for Christmas. At the same time, the Christmas season was officially established as the twelve days between December 25 and January 6. In the Holy Land, Christmas was celebrated on January 6, not December 25, because Palestine used the Egyptian calendar, which differed from the Roman. This lasted until about 650. Even though all Christians eventually settled on December 25, some cultures still mark January 6 with celebrations that rival those of Christmas.

In today's Italy, for instance, the presents do not come on December 25, but with the wise men on January 6, known as "little Christmas."

In addition to feast days, spirituality settled on certain devotions during these centuries, as well. Saints' relics followed in the tradition of martyrs' relics and especially appealed to new converts, who had a pre-Christian affinity for the sacredness of objects. The cross became the supreme wooden object of worship and was venerated as God's standard or staff, with poems dedicated to the cross's glory, such as the English *Dream of the Rood,* dating to the eighth century. Christ was often experienced spiritually as a stern judge because theologians continued to fight the remnants of Arianism (the fourth-century heresy that said Jesus was not divine) by emphasizing Christ's authority as the final arbiter of a Christian's fate. Marian devotion became even stronger after the Council of Ephesus in 431 declared clearly that Mary was the Mother of God (*Theotokos*), and not simply the mother of the human Jesus. This devotion grew especially in the eastern Mediterranean, where Mary was venerated poetically as the "earth unsown" and the "bridge leading to heaven."

In the East, one spiritual practice, the veneration of icons, led to conflict. Icons representing Jesus, Mary, and the saints were popular in the East, but starting in the seventh century iconoclasts defaced images because they felt no earthly object could properly reflect divinity or sanctity and were therefore idolatrous or heretical. After much violence in the Byzantine world (particularly in modern-day Turkey), the Second General

Council of Nicaea in 787 decreed that icons were appropriate and permitted: "...he who venerates the image, venerates the person represented in that image." Christians could express their spiritual devotion to Jesus, Mary, and the saints by lighting candles or burning incense before an icon, but they had to be taught and had to remember that the icon itself was not the object of ultimate belief or devotion—which had been the case with Greco-Roman pagan practices.

While Christianity developed in the East, where it had begun, spreading the faith northward in Europe presented a challenge. Evangelization was itself an act of spiritual devotion and action, but persistent pagan practices and ideas impeded the spread of Christian beliefs. A kind of synthesized spirituality emerged in central Europe, which blended Christianity with pagan practices, sometimes in a very thin line. When crops continually failed in Germany, for instance, a priest might combine honey, milk, or oil with soil and holy water, pray and say Masses over the mixture, and then have a Christian farmer sow what was essentially sanctified fertilizer into his fields. There were blessings for plows, weapons, and battlefield wounds; prayers against thunder and lightning, famine, illness, and difficult pregnancies; and relics to ward off toothaches and blindness. Prayers to the dead continued the cult of the martyrs and led to new saints, which in turn contributed to the feasts of All Souls and All Saints that would appear, with theological justifications and elaborate liturgies, shortly after the turn of the new millennium—yet another example of spirituality moving from the Church's body to her head for approval.

While some elements of these examples of spirituality and devotions may sound superstitious, they nevertheless indicate a measure of trust and faith on the part of both priest and lay person. Admittedly, everyday spirituality in this period was for the most part unlearned—especially to modern eyes—but not necessarily wrong. It may have been simple, but it was not simplistic, let alone misguided in its intentions. If spirituality was earthy, it was also essential and fixed on the right things: leading a faith-filled, good life in this world to prepare for the next.

The Medieval Church: Devotional Diversity

Spirituality flourished in the Middle Ages. There was diversity of devotions, and an upsurge in the use of vernacular languages across a spectrum of pious practices. A fundamental shift also occurred in the way people identified with Jesus, Mary, the saints, the Eucharist, and their Christian brothers and sisters at home. Spirituality changed dramatically because people began to see Jesus not as their final judge, but as a suffering, historical human being. With the final disappearance of Arianism, lay people and theologians grew more comfortable with the gentle Jesus of the Gospels, as they had been at the very beginning of Christianity a millennium before. Art, songs, sermons, and Passion plays depicted Jesus as the man of sorrows, humility, suffering, and service. The Christian could more easily identify with these aspects of Jesus than those of the glorified Son of God. This did not mean that people mistook Jesus for just another human. Rather, they understood how closely God was tied with their own difficult lives, especially the peasants, who struggled simply to live from day to day.

As a result, spirituality focused on Christ's passion and penitential actions whereby the Christian could imitate Christ in his suffering and charity, and on the Eucharist, through which Christians could experience the body of Christ. At times, excesses developed, however, when some people venerated "bleeding hosts" even after their bishops declared them to be suspect or fakes. The Gospel stories of Jesus became extremely popular, as did morality plays. These taught the lessons of Scripture or demonstrated how a local saint had followed Jesus' example in his or her own town and circumstances. Devotion to Mary logically grew, too, with Saturday being dedicated to her because she kept vigil and faith between Good Friday and Easter Sunday.

This focus on the Gospel made the devotions "evangelical" and practical. Francis of Assisi (ca. 1181–1226) became such a popular saint because in his humility, his poverty, and his stigmata, Francis embodied Christ. Francis set up the first Christmas crèche and living manger scene in Grecchio in 1223 in order to preach the Incarnation in a way that made sense visibly to his illiterate audience. The Franciscan Bonaventure (1217–1274), like many of his fellow preachers and theologians, guided his listeners and readers through vivid meditations. In them, he encouraged people to place themselves in a scene from the Gospel and ask what they would have done had they been right there with Jesus. Bonaventure and many other medieval authors wrote meditations on Christ's life, focusing especially on the passion, which led to the *imitatio Christi* spirituality. Medieval Christians looked around at their own situations and—800 years before today's Christians—asked, "What would Jesus do?"

It is not surprising, then, to find that pilgrimages to Jerusalem increased: Christians wanted to walk in the very footsteps of Christ. Because pilgrims faced great dangers on the journey, it became a metaphor for the pilgrim journey that every Christian takes on earth toward his or her heavenly destination. Pilgrims came home and set up small representations of the shrines they had seen connected to Jesus' passion. These developed into the Stations of the Cross for pilgrims who wanted to relive their journey, and also for those believers who would never be able to make the long, difficult, and expensive trip to the Holy Land. The Stations of the Cross gave them a spiritual practice at home that allowed them to walk with Christ through his last days on earth.

Spirituality was more active and apostolic than contemplative during the Middle Ages—at least for lay people. Spiritual activities often centered around confraternities, which were groups of like-minded people tied together by a region, a devotion (Corpus Christi or the Sacred Heart), or a profession (guilds). They engaged in cultural and charitable activities related to their common ground: carpenters, for example, would have a particular devotion to St. Joseph and serve their neighbors by building homes for the poor. Others joined "third orders": an attempt to find a middle or third way between living in a monastery or convent and the outside world. Lay people did not take formal vows proper to a religious order, but they became affiliated with a particular order and adopted its specific charism and spiritual activities into their daily lives.

While it may sound strange, death also became a specific devotion, but this makes sense since everyone must die, and a large part of the Christian life was devoted to preparing well in this world to live with God in the next. Medieval people took death very seriously, for it hung as a specter over their daily life. They had no drugs like penicillin, pregnancy often led to death, and common conditions like appendicitis could kill. Sermons and books encouraged the *ars moriendi*—the art of dying well. These directed people to live always in a state of grace and service so that they would be ready to meet God whenever death struck. Events like the Black Death from 1347 to 1351 or the "Hundred Years War" between England and France that started about that same time sharpened this awareness of death.

The *devotio moderna* or "modern devotion" exemplifies all of this spirituality. Centered in northern Europe among working-class lay people, this movement encouraged them to balance prayer life, spirituality, work, and family. Following the idea of a deacon named Geert Grote (ca. 1340–1384), they lived an apostolic life, but did not start a new religious order. Some men and women set up separate communities known as the Brothers and Sisters of the Common Life, but most lived at home and practiced these devotions. With activities that are striking because they resemble changes made after Vatican II, these lay people met in each other's homes to read the Bible and learn more about the faith. They translated parts of Scripture and the Mass into their Dutch dialect with their bishops' approval.

This popular piety for lay people focused on praying and keeping spiritual diaries, living the Gospel at home and work, examining their consciences daily, and identifying with Christ's suffering. They also worked to correct vices and develop virtues in concrete settings every day, not only on Sunday, and opposed rote devotions such as praying quickly or simply multiplying Our Fathers, hoping more will be better. A medieval story makes the point: a nun once fervently raced through 150 Hail Marys before a statue of Mary. When she finished, the statue miraculously spoke to her: "Just fifty prayers, Sister," Mary said, "but next time, with conviction."

The Reformation Church: Avoiding Excess

THE CHALLENGE FACING THE CHURCH on the eve of the Reformations was to take the best of the richness of medieval spirituality, but avoid the danger of arithmetical piety. One influential voice raised at this point in Church history came from the humanist Erasmus, who grew up in the same area in which the *devotio moderna* had flourished. Erasmus called people to practice the Christian virtues, but to live their active and apostolic spirituality according to the spirit and not the letter of the law. Formalism and counting good deeds had to give way to true, inward piety and charity that sprang from a desire to serve, not to gain indulgences for the sake of the person doing the good deed. Prayer, reading the Scriptures, learning the faith, and acting accordingly—this was the key to Erasmus' vision for spirituality and the renewal of the individual, the Church, and the world.

Much of the historical data about spirituality in late fifteenth and early sixteenth centuries comes from critics who tended to accentuate the negative. This makes it difficult to form a true picture of this era. Certainly, some people went to excess in their spirituality. Flagellants did not disappear and those seeking out witches or people practicing sorcery may have found what they were looking for, despite evidence to the contrary. A disordered love for Christ, overemphasis on his suffering, and a macabre fascination with his death could have promoted anti-Semitism. The urge to find a patron saint for every illness could have led to some bizarre devotions that had no basis in historical evidence or even legend. Some people seemed to act not to aid Christ in the least of their brothers and sisters, but just to collect indulgences so they could cut down the amount of time they might have to spend in purgatory. This led to a lively trade in phony relics, as readers of Chaucer's *Canterbury Tales* will recall. Stockpiling indulgences instead of growing spiritually is not what the Church had in mind.

At the same time, however, dissatisfaction with arithmetical piety and external actions also led to positive changes in spirituality during this period, which is probably the greatest moment in the history of mysticism. The famous sixteenth-century Spanish mystics Teresa of Avila, John of the Cross, and Ignatius Loyola led the way. Even those who did not reach their heights of mystical union with God strove to achieve important spiritual goals. They tried to move inwardly to the quiet of their hearts when activities relied too much on style and not enough on substance. Many lay people boosted their practice of the examination of their consciences and this led to some increase in the practice of confession. Lay confraternities proliferated and, while they tended to emphasize apostolic service, they also strongly focused on interior spiritual growth.

Movements for reform like this looked not to changing the system as much as to the way people exploited the system for the wrong reasons. While Martin Luther may have started from this position in 1517 with his *Ninety-Five Theses*, he quickly moved from fixing the Catholic system to abandoning large parts of it. When the Catholic Church finally responded after the long and intermittent Council of Trent adjourned in 1563, Catholics discovered that certain aspects of their spiritual exercises had been reemphasized, deemphasized, or channeled in renewed directions.

Many medieval types of spiritual activity continued in the Reformation period, but the Church monitored them more closely and brought them under greater supervision. Fear of superstition and heresy led to favoring unity and approved practices over diversity and innovation in spirituality. After Trent the trend toward interior spirituality continued. Catholics would imagine the life of Christ, put themselves into Gospel scenes, and try to figure out how to imitate Jesus in their own daily life. This emphasized that everyone, not just the clergy and the learned, were called to Christian perfection and the imitation of Christ. Spiritual directors helped people examine their consciences under clerical oversight and not their own. Spiritual direction made spirituality a bit more individual and not as communal as it sometimes had been in the Middle Ages, with public festivals that could get out of hand and lose their religious essence. Mysticism, the high point of interior spirituality, occasionally skirted the edges of institutional Church acceptance. This explains why some mystics—including Teresa, John, and Ignatius—were suspected of heresy, especially given the Protestant challenges in the sixteenth century and the medieval tradition of the Inquisition in their native Spain.

Trent mandated that parish priests must preach on every Sunday and holy day, which led many of them to bring the Gospels to life for their congregations and to promote more than ever the following of Jesus' apostolic example. Itinerant preaching missions also became a favorite spiritual activity. Offering simple and accessible catechism instead of university theology, the preachers led people back to the sacraments as a focus of their spiritual practices and to the core ideas of sin, judgment, repentance, and personal conversion. Parishes joined confraternities (now with greater clerical oversight) as centers of spiritual activities, which led to some loss of independence among lay people, but also to greater orthodoxy. What we might call "CCD" appeared late in the sixteenth century, with catechisms aimed at different professions, ages, and dialects. Local saints lost some ground to universal saints, such as Joseph and Anne. This move directed the people's spiritual practices toward exercises that all Catholics shared: work, parenthood, and scenes of Christ's life. To counter the Protestant de-emphasis of the Eucharist and the teaching of some Protestants that Jesus was not fully and forever present in the Eucharist, the Church stressed Eucharistic devotions, such as what became the Forty Hours and Perpetual Adoration. Devotion to the Sacred Heart of Jesus, identified as the very center of Christ's humanity and divinity, pointed out to Reformation Catholics that God should dwell in their own hearts, putting God and not themselves at the center of the spiritual life.

Finally, devotion to Mary increased dramatically, in part because of the Protestant charges that Mary had been made into a god. Not only did Catholics restate their Marian beliefs, but along with Eucharistic piety and activities, Marian devotions emerged from the Reformations as one of the major forms of spiritual activity. She was (and is), in a sense, "the" universal saint, because she transcends place, time, and culture. Confraternities distinguished by devotion to the Rosary grew, as did sermon and catechetical lessons on Mary and her example of obedience. A huge boost to Marian devotion came in 1572 when Pope Pius V (1566–1572) said that the Catholic victory over a Turkish fleet off the Greek coast the year before, called the Battle of Lepanto, had been assured through Mary's intervention. Right before the battle, sailors and soldiers on the many Catholic ships had together prayed the Rosary, shouting the prayers from one ship to the next. Pius V also established what became the feast of the Holy Rosary to commemorate this victory.

The Early Modern Church: Oversight and Expansion

EARLY MODERN SPIRITUALITY LARGELY followed the trends set by the Reformation period: an emphasis on individual spiritual progress, group activities increasingly supervised by the clergy, and a deepening and spreading of several popular devotions that held universal appeal. Authority to supervise spiritual activities fell largely to the bishops, who emerged from Trent as the key agents of reform and oversight. For example, all processions had to be led by priests in good standing with their bishop and religious superiors (if they belonged to religious orders). Although certain trends may predominate in spirituality in any age, some variety and adaptation also always occurs, especially when traditional devotions arrive in a new place such as the young United States.

While the focus on individual spiritual growth and examination of conscience became more common, sodalities and confraternities never lost their appeal. They not only joined Catholics together for mutual support, but also kept Catholics from slipping into Protestant denominations—or at least that's how some thinking went. The hierarchical Church especially promoted devotions that had wide and uniform appeal, rather than just local interest. This fact made groups focused on penitential activities (retreats, missions, and charitable service), the Eucharist, and the Rosary particularly popular for the people and attractive for the hierarchy. The Eucharist remained a key to all spirituality and members of all confraternities, regardless of their specific devotion, participated in Forty Hours' devotions, adoration, and Corpus Christi processions. Likewise, no matter what devotion one group favored, all members of confraternities and sodalities emphasized confession and communion as regular practices.

In the centuries after Trent we can note some changes in the understanding of sainthood, relics, and saints' cults. Mindful of some medieval superstitions, excesses, and misunderstandings, the early modern Church made it clear that saints do not perform miracles. God performs miracles, but can choose to act through the intercessions or actions of people whom the Church recognized as saints. New miracles and relics were permitted but, learning from the mistakes that both Erasmus and Luther had criticized, the Church retained the ultimate authority in deciding which miracles and relics were to be declared valid and worthy of devotion.

Spirituality related to the Virgin Mary continued to enjoy tremendous popularity and loyalty because of her universal appeal and the fact that championing Mary was a way of strongly asserting one's Catholicism. People talked about her Assumption in Marian congresses, prayed the Rosary, built chapels dedicated to her, and took vows in her name. St. Joseph, too, became popular, especially among laborers of the Industrial Revolution of the nineteenth century, who identified with his duty to work to support his family.

The emergence of romanticism as an artistic, cultural, and intellectual movement affected early modern spirituality, too. Within Catholicism, romanticism manifested itself in nostalgia (grounded more in myth than in reality) for a medieval Catholicism where Church and state were closely related and Catholicism had few challengers. People had a certain longing for an alleged golden age of medieval Christianity in which people's ultimate loyalty was to the Church, embodied by the pope. As we have already seen, this longing led to "ultamontanism," in which Catholics looked first to Rome for guidance, and they identified themselves first of all as Catholics. This was opposed to the nationalism that, in the 1800s, spurred people to classify themselves principally by ethnicity, culture, or language.

Romanticism and devotions to Mary and Jesus came together in the Sacred Heart devotion, which had begun to enjoy popularity during the Reformation era. Jesus' Sacred Heart, which became as favored an object of spirituality in the early modern Church as Jesus' broken body had been in the Middle Ages, showed God's love for everyone. It especially turned to Jesus' examples from the Gospels as well as the believers' emotional love for God as they sought to link their hearts with Christ's. The Immaculate Heart of Mary was closely related to the devotion to Jesus' Sacred Heart, which was often represented in affordable prints with a cross and crown of thorns to show the depth of Jesus' loving sacrifice.

European immigrants to America brought these devotions with them. In 1826, 250,000 Roman Catholics lived in the United States, but by the Civil War, thirty-five years later, they had grown to 3,000,000. The first large wave of Catholic immigrants came as a result of Ireland's potato famine in 1846, but in the century between 1820 and 1920, 1.7 million German Catholics arrived in the United States, plus several million southern Italians.

How did the American Catholic leadership respond? The first goal was to print a Catholic Bible for the largely Protestant country. This effort dated back to 1790, when a Philadelphia publisher put out the first Catholic Bible in the United States with the approval of Bishop John Carroll, the first Catholic bishop in the United States and a cousin of a Catholic signer of the Declaration of Independence. Catechisms and guides to prayer soon followed, often built around the very American themes of self-sufficiency and reason, but explicitly linked with God's grace, too.

Priests frequently emigrated with their congregations. Within cities, "national" parishes were established, such as German churches in Cincinnati and Polish parishes in Chicago. Their spirituality reminded them of home, with great attention paid to the familiar rituals that eased homesickness and could travel with them: Marian devotions, Eucharistic adoration, and Sacred Heart confraternities. They also established new feasts, like New York City's San Gennaro festival, and replanted favorite saints, like St. Patrick in Manhattan. At the same time, Catholics from different countries could mingle in America, especially in revival missions held in cities and the countryside by religious orders such as the Redemptorists and Paulists, who made sure to keep people close to the sacraments no matter how far they might be from their homelands.

The Modern Church: The Old and the New

MANY VARIED SPIRITUALITIES ENRICH the modern Church. Devotions such as Eucharistic adoration and the Rosary have found a renewed popularity following a slight decline after Vatican II. Now they are attracting a new audience in a younger generation of Catholics who were not raised with these practices. At the same time, the trend that developed after Vatican II to experiment with Eastern religions continues, but the historical caveat of syncretism remains: Catholic spirituality must not adapt so much to other traditions that it loses its essence. This means that the last 150 years or so of Church history have witnessed continued testing and adaptation while spirituality grounded in the past also remains popular.

Catholic spirituality in the United States is a particularly good example of these parallel developments. While shrines at martyrs' graves began very early in Church history, America did not have ancient Christian places to visit. So new shrines modeled on Mediterranean and European sites began to sprout up across the country. For example, the University of Notre Dame built a replica of the Lourdes shrine on its campus in 1877, complete with water imported from Lourdes itself. By the early twentieth century, North American destinations attracted pilgrims: a shrine to Our Lady of Sorrows in Missouri, for instance, and another in Auriesville, New York, to the Jesuit missionary martyrs who worked there and in French Canada. Throughout the country, processions and feasts, often associated with Holy Week, were transplanted from the

"Old World" (especially Italy and Spain) to the "New World" (particularly in North American cities). All of these gave focus to immigrant spirituality and helped American Catholics mold an identity.

American devotionalism peaked from the 1920s to the 1950s, with rosaries, annual May crownings of Our Lady, Forty Hours' devotions (popular specifically among Polish Catholics), and frequent novenas. Catholic publishers supported these forms of spirituality by supplying affordable prayer books, spiritual readers, magazines, and pamphlets. Missions and retreats flourished, especially retreats for men, which were often linked to the Holy Name Society or the Knights of Columbus. Every house had a crucifix, statues, spiritual reading materials, and a print of the pope—as the papacy itself was beginning to become an object of devotion and spirituality for many Catholics.

Spirituality took a very activist turn in the late nineteenth century, especially when Pope Leo XIII wrote the encyclical *Rerum Novarum* in 1891, which called for fair wages, good working conditions, and even government aid to working families. These spiritual and practical concerns, often grouped under the heading of social justice, were in part a reaction to the degradations that workers suffered under the nineteenth-century's Industrial Revolution. In Europe, this activist spirituality cohered around a movement called Catholic Action, which operated formally and informally, but usually under the guidance of the local bishop. Popes Pius X (1903–1914) and Pius XI (1922–1939) both enthusiastically supported Catholic

Action, especially in the efforts of lay people to do charitable service in cooperation with the Church's hierarchy. In the United States, Dorothy Day (1897–1980) and the Catholic Worker movement, established in 1933, linked American Catholicism to the social justice movement. Starting with the Depression's soup kitchens, it emphasized Christ living in each working and poor individual.

Marian spirituality remained very strong throughout the world in the modern period, but especially in the very troubled first half of the twentieth century. Devotion to Our Lady of Guadalupe had flourished since the seventeenth century in Mexico, and it grew quickly wherever Spanish-speaking people emigrated around the globe in the twentieth century. Shrines to Our Lady began to spring up all over the world in the modern period: in France at Là Salette (1846) and Lourdes (1858), for example, and then in Ireland at Knock (1879). Piety associated with Our Lady of Fatima began in 1917 and won papal approval in 1942. Decades before World War II, however, Marian spirituality was tied closely with prayers to fight Communism. Marian devotions are strongly linked to John Paul II, both for his very strong personal devotion to Mary and his own fight against Communism. This began during his years as a priest, bishop, and cardinal in Poland, then continued in his support of the Polish Solidarity movement shortly after his 1978 election. This in turn helped lead to Communism's total collapse in 1989 and the next few years. But John Paul II was not the first pope in this period to honor Mary. Pope

Pius IX defined the Immaculate Conception in 1854; Leo XIII wrote eleven documents on the Rosary; and Pius XII consecrated the world to Mary's Immaculate Heart in 1942, proclaimed a Marian year in 1945, and defined the Assumption in 1950.

After Vatican II, many devotions that were familiar to an older generation of Catholics—May crownings, novenas, Forty Hours' devotion, perpetual adoration, and others—fell out of favor during a period of liturgical and spiritual renewal and innovation. As a result, these devotions were often called "traditional," a word sometimes intended to indicate spiritual actions that were either outdated and should be left behind, or that were worthy and were unfairly cast aside. So "traditional devotions" have become controversial, with proponents and opponents lining up against each other. This situation is extremely unfortunate, since spirituality has always been a very individual and personal way of exercising the faith. Variety has usually been appreciated as a rich heritage of Catholic life. Viewed in this light, it is interesting to see the return and rising popularity of "traditional devotions" like Perpetual Adoration and the Rosary among different generations of Catholics. Hopefully it is not simply nostalgia that brings them back, but an appreciation that these longstanding spiritualities have a place in the Vatican II Church, too.

Chapter 8

RELIGIOUS ORDERS

How did religious orders develop?

The Early Church: Asceticism

Religious orders, as we know them today, took quite some time to develop. If we look at the Church's earliest centuries, we will uncover only traces of their beginnings. Because Christianity was illegal in the Roman Empire for the first few centuries of her life, standard and organized developments did not exist. Instead, during the Church's first 400 years, various types of religious life emerged. Gradually they became the religious orders that we will recognize more clearly later in Church history.

The first aspect of religious life we see is a strict, austere attempt to live Christian ideals away from the larger society. Many scholars of religion have pointed out that there will always be members of a particular faith who choose to live apart and pursue religious perfection as directly and vigorously as possible. This may have happened with Christianity in part because some Christians withdrew from the sometimes-hostile pagan, Roman society around them to avoid physical persecution and spiritual contamination. We find a good example in Antony of Alexandria (251–256) in Egypt, although he is surely not the first to live a strict lifestyle. He abandoned his family's comfortable circumstances, withdrew to the desert, and lived alone to pray and work with his hands.

As often happens, he drew supporters, admirers, and pupils who wished to learn from him, which ironically made his solitary life a bit busy at times. Some of these pupils took up residence near his own small hut. This resulted in communities of a few ascetics living nearby, meeting perhaps for Sunday Eucharist and to encourage each other in the tough life they were leading. The individuals were known as anchorites or even monks (though not in a medieval or modern sense) and lived mainly as hermits in an eremitical lifestyle. These were overwhelmingly male individuals and communities, given the social challenges for a woman living alone during this period. Nevertheless, groups of rich women, especially virgins and widows, did withdraw into country villas to pray, study Scripture, and practice a measure of asceticism such as fasting. Some of them, drawn by Jerome (342–420), even moved to Jerusalem and Bethlehem and went on to establish communities of women there. But we do not find many individual ascetical women in the East, unless they traveled there from the West, and women almost certainly did not withdraw to deserts or caves.

As Christianity became more tolerated, accepted, and then mandated as the only religion in the Roman Empire, the solitary holy Christian replaced the martyr as the Church's hero. Communities of ascetics developed particularly in the deserts of Palestine, Syria, and Egypt. We also find hermits living just as harshly in the rocky caves of the Alps, southern Italy, and modern-day Turkey. Of course, even this already-harsh lifestyle had its extremists: some tied themselves to trees (dendrites) or lived on top of tall columns (stylites). While these attracted attention in their own time—and ours—they were only a distinct minority.

Individuals living relatively close to each other formed cenobitical or communal groups, which in turn led to the need for some type of organizing principle or rule. Pachomius (286–346) was the first to write such a rule in which he stressed the importance of communal activity and support. For Pachomius, prayer and work could be useful and not simply penitential, which led to more practical forms of monasticism. Basil the Great (329–379) followed with another rule, but John Cassian (360–435) merged East and West. Born in the Balkans, he spent ten years living the desert experience in the East, including a year in Bethlehem. He then brought his experiences to Gaul in 395, where he established St. Savior monastery for women and St. Victor for men. Emphasizing detachment and a certain puritanical asceticism, Cassian produced one book titled *Conferences,* which conveyed sayings and stories of the Egyptian desert fathers, and another book titled the *Institutes,* which explained the customs of the cenobitical lifestyle. These became the handbooks of religious life in this period.

When we look at these origins and first principles of religious life, their rigor stands out. One of the values these earliest religious "orders" held was *apatheia,* which was a Greek notion of being dead to the world by not giving in to passions, emotions, or lusts. A Latin, medieval mind would refer to this as *contemptus mundi,* or contempt for/turning away from the world. We cannot deny this tendency, but we must remember two things. First, these earliest "monks" and "nuns"—to be dangerously anachronistic—lived in the shadow of persecution, since they began to withdraw from their communities during Roman persecutions in the third century. They believed they were being purified in the face of what might cause their imminent deaths. Second, the literature that comes down to us as the sayings or proverbs of the desert fathers and mothers is surely exaggerated to clearly and dramatically make their points about purging souls.

These sayings and pieces of spiritual advice emphasized order and discipline, which acted as the foundation of a method that prepared ascetics to receive God's grace and enjoy spiritual communion with God. An ascetic's discipline, enforced by him- or herself or others, allowed him or her to abandon earthly concerns to focus on spiritual matters. Bodily mortification took the form of fasting from food, wine, sex, and sleep. As an abbot named Daniel advised, "When the body flourishes, the soul withers, and when the body withers, the soul blossoms." One story is told of a group of religious women walking on a road when an ascetic man stepped aside to let them pass. Their abbess was not impressed: "If you were a perfect monk," she told him, "you would not have noticed that we were women." Probably few ascetics reached this highest level of "death to the world." But many earnest men and women did strive to come close to God in their lives by focusing entirely on their relationship with God even during these first hazardous centuries for Christianity.

The First Millennium Church: Moderation

RELIGIOUS ORDERS CAME INTO THEIR OWN during this period, leading to several developments and responses.

First, the early Church's extreme asceticism and individuality continued and became a problem, especially in Ireland. Second, and in reaction, the giant of religious life emerged: Benedict of Nursia (480–550). He organized, modified, and smoothed out the extremes of religious life with his foundational and enormously influential *Rule*. Third, during the 500 years after Benedict, monasteries sometimes became not oases from the world, but institutions closely controlled by rich lay people. They wanted to benefit from the monasteries' economic potential and cared little for the spiritual progress of the monks and nuns. So a counteraction to this control rose up in a reform of monastic life led by the French monastery of Cluny. We'll look at each of these in turn.

First, Irish monasticism was highly individual and sometimes extreme, following the lead of the East. Highly charismatic Irish abbots often wielded more power than bishops, because abbots were related to the Irish clan structure. Irish monasticism stressed penitential practices: long fasts, prayers said for hours (sometimes in icy water) while the monks or nuns held their arms out in a cruciform, many prostrations and genuflections. Confession was frequent, sometimes daily. But the Irish monks and nuns knew something very important: extreme solitude did not mean loneliness as long as they established companionship with God.

Second, Benedict of Nursia applied his classical Roman education to religious life after he converted to Christianity around the year 500. In part, he wanted to respond to the extremist trend that sometimes led to eccentricity and a lack of obedience. Using his monastery at Monte Cassino, north of Naples, as an experimental lab, around 530 he wrote his *Rule,* drawing on earlier rules and experience. It soon became the guide for religious life for 500 years and beyond. The *Rule* made religious life more practical, more flexible, and better adapted to each particular monastery and to each monk or nun's individual temperament. Benedict carefully structured the daily life of the cenobitical community by emphasizing moderation, balance, and discretion. A monastery's residents made three promises—which would not formally develop into the vows of poverty, chastity, and obedience until the thirteenth century. Monks and nuns promised to be stable and rooted in one community instead of wandering around, as happened in the East and Ireland. They promised to devote themselves to their personal *metanoia,* or a fundamental change in the way they lived their lives for God. They also promised to obey their superiors, especially the abbot and abbess, who stood in God's place. It is important to remember that most men in the monasteries were still not priests but lay people, which had been the case from religious life's first centuries.

Benedict's other great contributions involved prayer and work. He fixed the hours of prayer into eight periods: Matins (about 2 A.M.), Lauds (5 A.M.), Prime (6 A.M., to match the Roman "first" hour of the day), Terce (9 A.M., or the "third" hour), Sext (noon, the sixth hour), None (3 P.M., the ninth hour), Vespers (about 4 P.M.), and Compline (sunset or right before bedtime, typically between 5 and 8 P.M., depending on location and season). Benedict believed prayer was the essential "work" of the Church, hence the phrase *opus Dei* or "work of God" (which does not refer here to the modern religious association). He taught that the choir of monks or nuns, when praying or singing, should recreate the choir of angels who sing God's praises constantly. Benedict also required private prayer and reading (*lectio divina*) and significantly transformed the idea of manual labor, which the Romans had disdained as slaves' or women's work. In Benedict's mind, work gave the monks and nuns a necessary break from prayer and made the monastery self-sufficient. It allowed monks and nuns to participate in God's creative power by gardening to produce food, copying manuscripts to hand along God's Word, or making furniture or clothing. For Benedict, work led to sanctification no less than prayer did.

We come to the third development of this period. In the half-millennium after Benedict, monastery life sometimes devolved. Benedict envisioned communities of one or two dozen with a leader who could personally know each monk or nun. Monasteries grew to include hundreds. Also, abbots and abbesses were not independently elected by their monks or nuns as the *Rule* mandated, but were appointed by the richest local lay leader, who often chose a relative with no interest in the spiritual guidance of the community's members. Subsequently, the religious life of the monasteries crumbled: the hours of prayer were neglected, monks and nuns did not stay in their monasteries, and they showed little concern for spiritual growth and discipline. In response, a layman, Duke William of Aquitaine, established the monastery at Cluny in 910. The duke had committed murder, repented, and wanted to do some good. The first abbot, named Berno, was strong enough to make the penitent William agree that Cluny would be exempt from all secular authority and subject directly to the pope (because a lay man often appointed the local bishop or abbot). This insured that Cluny could freely elect its own abbot.

Because of a period of relative peace and stability, Cluny prospered and became an attractive model of reformed Benedictine life. Before long, hundreds of monasteries had adopted its plan and "Cluniac" monasteries arose across Europe. The abbot of Cluny became the second most powerful cleric in Christian Europe, second only to the pope in Rome. The abbot wielded a huge amount of influence over all the other monasteries affiliated with the Cluniac reforms. Religious life was restored with increased splendor: art and architecture were made more ornate, liturgies grew nearly theatrical, and only the best fabrics and metals were used for the Mass's vestments and vessels. At the same time, however, asceticism, discipline, simplicity, and poverty declined from Benedict's standards. Many more monks than before were ordained, since benefactors wanted Masses said for their souls in perpetuity. A split developed between an upper level of "choir monks" who prayed and said Mass and a lower level of illiterate lay brothers. These were deprived of equal status and did the sanctifying manual labor Benedict had required of every monk and nun. As the first millennium concluded, then, we see developments that held within themselves both positive and negative aspects for religious life.

The Medieval Church: Reform

IN THE MIDDLE AGES RELIGIOUS COMMUNITIES experienced both reaction and innovation. Not only did yet another type of Benedictine monasticism react to a prior form, but a new way of living religious life emerged as well: the mendicant lifestyle of the Franciscan and Dominican friars. Let us begin with a link to the past before seeing how the mendicants moved toward the future.

Even though Cluny itself had begun as a reform movement against lay control, a counter movement emerged that sought to return Benedictine monasticism to its roots. Some monks and nuns reacted against what they saw as Cluniac excesses. This movement took two forms: the Carthusians and the Cistercians. While they differ somewhat, both the Carthusians and Cistercians reacted negatively to Cluny's elaborate rituals, large monastic houses, and wealth. The Carthusians, the more austere of the two, were begun by a monk named Bruno (1030–1101). After a distinguished teaching career, Bruno gathered a few friends to take up a highly eremitical lifestyle in an isolated monastery ultimately named, rather colorfully, La Grande Chartreuse. Bruno designed it specifically to recall Benedict of Nursia's small plan. Each monk had an individual cell with a private garden, a workshop, a water source, and a room in which to pray and sleep. Each small monastery that followed usually had one abbot or abbess and a dozen monks or nuns. Bruno returned the *opus Dei* to a simple chant, with only Matins, Lauds, and Vespers said in common, like the original ascetical communities of hermits that gathered only occasionally for Mass and communal support. He also restored manual labor for all monks, recognizing its power for spiritual sanctity, and he reemphasized *lectio divina*.

Because of its austerity, the Carthusians grew slowly, but the Cistercians—who agreed with the Carthusian return to simplicity, but not quite as drastically—spread quickly. Like the Carthusians, the first Cistercians aimed at fidelity to Benedict's *Rule*. Robert of Molesme (1028–1112) was the Cistercian founding abbot. In 1098, he and about twenty monks found an isolated, wooded area that approximated in Europe the isolation the desert fathers had sought 800 years before in Egypt and Palestine. Another key figure, Stephen Harding (ca. 1060–1134), who had assisted Robert at the beginning, explained the Cistercians' reasons for setting themselves up in the careful way that they did—in essence becoming a sort of Benedict for his organizational abilities. Like the Carthusians, the Cistercians sought a return to the *Rule* as a means to spiritual ends, to poverty and simplicity (especially in liturgy, architecture, and Mass vestments and vessels), to the spirituality of manual labor, and to the spirituality of solitude.

At nearly the same time that the Cistercians were gaining members quickly and the Carthusians were finding their own followers, medieval Europe was changing rapidly. Agricultural advancements allowed more people to live in cities without producing their own food, so towns were growing and urban university life competed with rural monastic libraries as places of learning. As always happens, as the rich got richer, the poor got poorer and were often neglected. Meanwhile, some bishops and popes acquired more power and became bureaucratic, sometimes even wealthy and worldly. The Church needed a way of responding to these new urban needs, especially of the poor, and of returning the Church to the purity, poverty, and direct service of the Gospels. Enter Francis and Dominic.

We must view Francis (ca. 1181–1226) and Dominic (1170–1221) in their medieval context in order to understand their place in history. In Francis' case especially, none of the existing religious communities suited his ideas for the radical living out of the Gospel among the people in whom Christ dwelt. This is not to criticize monks and nuns who prayed, but Francis wanted to live more like Martha than Mary. After rejecting his family's wealth, he felt a call to renew the Church in a new way and not just by adapting what was already available, such as the various versions of monasticism. Francis resisted starting a new religious community and took the Gospels as his "rule," partly because his simplicity and lack of learning clashed with a Church milieu that was increasingly scholastic and legalistic. He eventually collaborated on a *Rule* that fit into the structure, organization, and legal language required by canon lawyers. He amended this *Rule* late in his life with some final instructions called his *Last Will and Testament*. But his essential vision, that of the mendicant way, transformed the history of religious life.

It is essential to remember that Francis and Dominic wanted a completely different type of religious community: one that was not tied to a physical place, like a monastery, but was open to apostolic service wherever needed. They especially favored working in the ghettos and town squares where Jesus was to be found among the least of his brothers and sisters. They also saw that they needed to be flexible, available, and in tune with the times, even while keeping the traditional ways of religious life connected to poverty, chastity, and obedience. They never abandoned the importance of prayer, which they said in a choir stall or while walking on a road. Some Franciscans got bogged down in debates over poverty to the point where, shortly after Francis' death, the order split into factions. The Dominicans, meanwhile, were more successful in maintaining unity and seeing poverty as a means, not an end, and avoiding some of the extremes into which a group of Franciscans fell.

A critical difference was that Dominic embraced university training more than Francis did, although within a century Franciscans would play an important role in medieval university life. At the start of the members' careers, Dominic saw theological study as the key to fighting learned heresies and their many followers. Dominic knew that he needed to fight heretics on their own turf and with their own tools, especially preaching. So he made sure that the members of his religious community, the Dominicans, studied theology to debate heretics. But he also wanted them to preach to the masses; since so many people could not read, they had to be persuaded by what they heard. In fact, the Dominicans had more priests than any other medieval religious order. In part, this was because Dominic and the Dominican leaders who succeeded him realized that the prestige of priesthood would help them in their tasks of preaching, teaching, and reconciling fallen-away Christians. Francis and Dominic, therefore, read the signs of the times and created new ways to respond to new challenges, even while other groups reached back in Church history to revitalize older forms of religious life that had lost their way.

The Reformation Church: Response

ALTHOUGH AT THE TIME THE REFORMATION may have seemed to bring tremendous threats and dangers, in retrospect we can see the period as one of innovation for religious orders. Both male and female communities had to respond to change and challenge.

Opportunities for women in religious orders in the Reformation (and the Middle Ages before that) varied. For centuries, some women had been placed in convents, even though they may not have had a religious vocation, simply because their parents could not afford a dowry (although some convents required or requested a kind of dowry payment). Others saw the convent as a place where they could exercise influence, authority, and a measure of independence, given their limited chances to do so in the outside world. When the

Protestant reformers abolished religious orders, women in Protestant territories lost ground. Even as some Protestant reformers proclaimed the priesthood of all believers, the power of patriarchy increased in Protestant countries. Virginity went from virtue to vice: nuns and novices were accused of turning their backs on the role of wife and mother in the household. Some convents were attacked physically, with the women being turned out shouting that their vocations were being violated. Some were stripped of their habits, and worse. The most famous attacks on both male and female houses occurred when King Henry VIII dissolved all religious houses in England beginning in 1536, in part to gain their wealth for himself. They all disappeared within just four years.

For centuries, nuns had a much higher literacy rate than women outside the convent because of the requirements of *opus Dei* and *lectio divina*. As with men, however, convents sometimes had a two-tiered system of elite or aristocratic nuns and "worker bees" of a lower status. At least this upper level could read, write, and even teach within the convent walls, although the social status of women denied them the physical freedom of wandering as mendicants. A 1298 Church regulation called *Periculoso* mandated strict cloistering and male oversight of women in religious life. About a decade later, this restriction was extended to women who lived a sort of monastic life as lay women usually called tertiaries or beguines. The Council of Trent in the sixteenth century reiterated this cloister rule, although it was not universally applied. For women, then, the cloister brought both opportunity and challenge.

Starting in the later Middle Ages and building through the Reformation period, many "observantine" movements sprang up in religious orders. They sought to return to their roots, to discard any accretions that had clouded their original charisms (guiding spirits), and to embrace a world now split between Catholics and Protestants. Typically, these observantine movements operated within versions of three existing orders: Benedictines, who often returned to enclosure; Augustinians, who sought a middle way between the cloister and the world; and the mendicant Franciscans and Dominicans, who lived fully in the world. The reformed or "observant" Franciscans, for example, became the Capuchins and rededicated themselves to poverty, simple service, and preaching, specifically among the rural poor. Luther himself was a monk of a German observantine Augustinian community. Perhaps the other best-known reform is that of the Carmelite order led by Teresa of Avila (1515–1582) and John of the Cross (1542–1591), who established the Discalced Carmelites.

New times led to entirely new religious orders, as well. The two best examples are the female Ursulines and the male Jesuits, neither of which existed before the Reformation. The Ursulines trace their beginnings to Angela Merici (1474–1540) and took their name from St. Ursula, the patron saint of education in the Middle Ages. Merici dedicated her group to the task of education, especially catechesis in light of the

Protestant criticisms, often well founded, that Catholics did not know their faith. The Ursulines believed quite correctly that women were (and remain) often the first teachers of children in the faith. Ursulines sought to renew the Church from the bottom up by educating poor girls about Christianity; indeed, wherever women were educated, the Church's reform flourished.

Although they started as a loose federation of individuals, each of whom still lived at home with their families, eventually they gathered into a community and took vows. This move came under the patronage of the great reforming bishop Charles Borromeo, a model for other bishops, who recognized the Ursulines' skills and achievements. He gave them protection and prestige by inviting them to his large diocese of Milan, but they struggled at times because of Trent's rule of enclosure. The Ursulines could not do their jobs behind closed doors, so a few decades of negotiation ensued whereby the Ursulines accepted a measure of male oversight while gaining some freedom to teach outside the cloister. Angela Merici had the genius to make sure her community could always adapt. As she instructed the community in one of its documents, "If according to times and needs you should be obliged to make fresh rules and change certain things, do it with prudence and on good advice."[1]

The Jesuits, meanwhile, decided that the best way to renew the Church was to educate the best-and-the-brightest boys, who were often wealthy. They believed these boys would become the next generation's leaders. The Jesuits also did other work besides education.

Ignatius Loyola (1491–1556) started his "company" shortly after Luther's challenge. Ignatius saw the need for a new type of priest who spent much time on education, winning Protestants back to the Catholic fold and spreading the faith in the new missions that followed Columbus' voyages at the end of the fifteenth century. Like Angela Merici, Ignatius clearly tapped into an important need. Less than a century after his death, over 500 Jesuit schools of various levels had sprung up, many of them free, rigorous, and illustrious.

Among the many other innovations, one other group merits our attention. As with Teresa of Avila and John of the Cross, we again find a pairing of a creative woman and man. Francis de Sales (1567–1622), the bishop of Geneva, founded the Order of the Visitation of Holy Mary as a result of his spiritual direction and friendship with Jane Frances de Chantal (1572–1641). De Chantal's husband had died after just seven years of marriage, leaving her with four children. After several years of discussion, in 1610 de Sales and de Chantal jointly started the order specifically for women who could not join a traditional cloister because of age, health, or other circumstances—such as de Chantal's own situation. Once again, new circumstances led some to think outside the proverbial box and offer a changing world new models of living a religious life. This type of pragmatism would expand all the more in the early modern Church.

The Early Modern Church: Innovation

BUILDING ON THE NEW CHALLENGES posed by both the Reformation and the discovery of territories beyond Europe, religious orders flourished. In Protestant territories in Europe, the remnants of some orders, especially women, did the best they could under the circumstances. They lived off the charity of their families in rented rooms, even though they could not always wear their habits, live in community, or pray together. Others joined the Jesuits in smuggling themselves into England to minister to the underground Catholic community after Queen Elizabeth fully turned to Protestantism by establishing the Anglican Church and outlawing the Catholic Church. European convents became places for prayer and support of the conflicts between Catholics and Protestants, centers to train missionaries, retreat houses for women, and catechetical schools.

But their fortunes turned to the worse again in the seventeenth and eighteenth centuries. The Enlightenment and then the French Revolution led to further physical attacks against convents, even in Catholic countries. The revolutionaries saw convents as places of elitism, and the *intelligentsia* disdained religious women as superstitious. Many nuns went to the guillotine rather than give up their religious vows. In 1792, in a replay of what had occurred 250 years before in England, religious houses were dissolved in France. As Napoleon advanced through Europe, convents in Belgium, Germany, and Italy suffered the same fate. All these factors combined to turn the eyes of religious orders to America, which promised more and greater opportunities—and fewer impediments.

Groups of nuns, led once more by the cutting-edge Ursulines, headed first for New Orleans and Quebec. Others left Europe's religious communities and cloisters, quickly following explorers and male missionaries (themselves nearly always members of religious orders). They began to teach in schools run by French, Spanish, and Portuguese Jesuits, Dominicans, Franciscans, and Augustinians in what eventually became Canada, the southwest United States, Mexico, as well as various Caribbean and Central and South American countries. They arrived also in Indonesia, Greece, Africa, and Australia. For women especially, these "new worlds" represented some freedom from enclosure. But even in the United States, where anti–immigration feelings often focused on Catholics (especially Irish and Germans in the nineteenth century), nuns were not immune from attack. Most notably, their convents in Baltimore, St. Louis, and Charlestown, Massachusetts, were assaulted and even burned in the 1830s. Still, these nuns continued to teach and especially to reach out to the poor and working classes. In the United States and Europe they ministered to those who were the castoffs of the Industrial Revolution's factory and class systems. Like the medieval mendicants, they were reading the signs of the times, responding in new ways, and radically living the Gospel.

Some of the more innovative religious orders that came into existence to meet these challenges were the Christian Brothers, and the Daughters and Sisters of

Charity of the Vincentian tradition. Once more, we find a partnership of a man and woman: Vincent de Paul (1581–1660) and Louise de Marillac (1591–1660). Together they established in 1633 a community of nuns that came to be known as the Daughters of Charity, whose many affiliates throughout the world took the name Sisters of Charity. They were not cloistered because, as de Paul said, the city streets were their cloisters. In the United States, Elizabeth Bayley Seton (1774–1821) took up the Vincentian charism by setting up a boarding school for girls in Baltimore in 1808. But her fascinating story begins earlier than that. Like Jane Frances de Chantal, Seton was a widowed mother; when she was twenty-nine her husband died, leaving her with five children under the age of eight. After living in Italy for a while, she converted to Catholicism in 1805. She became the first native-born American declared a saint when Pope Paul VI canonized her in 1975, which was also the International Year of the Woman. Mother Seton began what is really the first American religious community, and affiliates of the Sisters of Charity followed throughout the United States and Canada. In addition, building perhaps unintentionally on the Ursuline tradition, Mother Seton started the parochial school system that remains the envy of school systems around the globe, beginning with the education of young girls who would lead the domestic church in their homes.

The education of boys, meanwhile, remained important not only with the ongoing efforts of the Jesuits, but with a new group: the Christian Brothers.

Shortly after de Paul and de Marillac died, John Baptist de la Salle (1651–1719), like the medieval Francis of Assisi, walked away from his family's wealth and turned to working with the poor in France. After gathering a few companions, which often happens with a forward-thinking and charismatic religious person, about a dozen men joined de la Salle in what would become the Brothers of the Christian Schools in 1686. The Brothers specifically wanted to push religious life ahead and not simply recreate an existing order. The key was their companionship in living and teaching together in a manner that was not strictly "monastic" or "mendicant" in the traditional terms. They were to be brothers, not priests, and their schools continue to be a vital part of American Catholic education.

Despite being a relatively secular moment in European and American history, the middle of the nineteenth century witnessed large increases in membership in religious orders. By one count almost 125 congregations for women were established worldwide between 1850 and 1865, although the overwhelming majority were new houses of existing orders. Nevertheless, the witness of creative women like Mother Seton and men like John Baptist de la Salle demonstrate that religious orders continued to respond to changing times to renew the Church.

The Modern Church: Updating

IN THE LATE NINETEENTH AND EARLY twentieth centuries, membership in existing religious orders exploded. For example, worldwide the number of Salesians quadru-pled to 3,500 members from 1888 to 1914. There were 1,600 Benedictines in 1850, but 6,000 just fifty years later. The Trappists, with roots in Europe's Cistercian houses, tripled to 3,700 members between 1850 to 1900. The Jesuits had less than 5,000 members before the American Civil War, but almost 17,000 by the time World War I began in 1914.

The pressing need for teachers in the missions spurred this growth. Pope Pius IX (1846–1878) called on all religious orders to send members to mission ter-ritories to help educate and evangelize indigenous pop-ulations. Philadelphia's Mother Drexel responded by organizing schools in the West for Native Americans beginning in 1891. In the United States, teachers were also needed for the continuous waves of immigrants. From the Irish and German in the early and mid-nine-teenth century to the Italians and Slavs in the late nine-teenth and early twentieth centuries, large numbers of Catholics arrived in the United States. Religious com-munities often accompanied immigrants across the Atlantic, settled with them in industrial cities, and then moved with them to suburban and rural areas. Moreover, in the United States, religious orders added to their traditional tasks of teaching immigrants by staffing schools set up for emancipated slaves in Florida, Georgia, and Maryland after the Civil War.

One way of measuring the vitality of these religious orders is to look at the number of American parochial schools. Members of religious orders staffed almost all of them. In 1858, a gathering of bishops from the Midwest in Cincinnati declared that every pastor must build a parochial school "under pain of mortal sin." By 1865, 75 percent of parishes in New York City had schools, primarily for Irish and German Catholics. In 1875, there were 1,400 parochial schools in the United States. Less than a decade later, that number had grown to 2,500, mainly in urban areas. Many churches and parish schools were located within several blocks of each other. This building occurred in response to the Cincinnati meeting and also to the Third Plenary Council of Baltimore in 1884. America's bishops met there and mandated that every church have a school nearby. Earlier that century, New York's very powerful Archbishop John Hughes (nicknamed "Dagger John" because he fought so strongly for Catholics) had declared remarkably, "Build the schoolhouse first and the church afterward."[2]

Central diocesan school boards followed in the next several decades. These offices represented more chances for men and women in religious orders to exercise authority and leadership. Teachers needed training, as well. Despite the caricature of the nasty nun striking students on their hands with rulers, many teaching nuns (and brothers) earnestly dedicated themselves to their classroom efforts. Not every order, however, spent as much time in teacher training as in inculturating novices to the charism, history, and spirituality of their particular orders. Still, a need for education was met in summer institutes, starting in the 1910s at the Catholic University of America in Washington, D.C., and spreading to women's colleges across the country. When state certification standards rose in the 1920s and 1930s, many more nuns were sent for classes, typically over the many summers it took for them to finish bachelor's and master's degrees and teaching certificates.

The many schools and students needed teachers. But, in fact, that policy of building churches and schools in the cities where poor and working-class Catholics lived around 1850–1950 is now causing problems in American dioceses. Today's bishops are forced to close urban schools and parishes, but open them in the suburbs and rural areas around cities where upwardly mobile Catholics have moved. At the same time, Catholic parochial schools are educating immigrants as they have always done. But these immigrants are not always Catholic and many schools have no religious sisters or brothers teaching in them any longer. From the nineteenth century, parochial schools had been built with the idea that religious orders would staff them and so they did not need competitive salaries for their teachers. As membership in religious communities has declined, the financial situation of parochial schools has suffered. However, demographics and economics, not people, are largely to blame.

The decline in membership seems to be an unintended consequence of the social, political, and religious revolutions of the 1960s, in which Vatican II played a principal role. Many members of religious orders expressed dissatisfaction either with what they saw as the slowness or inadequacy of changes after the council or, on the other hand, the very changes themselves that so radically altered the lives they had been leading for decades. Vatican II must be seen as yet another challenge and opportunity for religious communities. The council's documents called on orders to rediscover the charism of their founders, many of whom had lived centuries before in very different circumstances, and to renew and adapt that charism for the modern contexts in which they lived:

> The sensitive renewal of religious life involves: the constant return to the sources of Christian life in general, and the original genius of religious foundations in particular; together with the modifications of such foundations to accommodate new circumstances.... It is to the Church's great advantage that each religious foundation has its particular spirit and function. Each must, therefore, reverence and embrace the genius and directives of its founder, its authentic traditions, the whole heritage, indeed, of the religious body. (*Perfectae caritatis,* no. 2)

Most obviously, this led to changes in religious habits, and people still remember what is was like to realize for the first time that Sister had legs, feet, and hair. But while this may be a favorite memory, it is largely not important. More important is the fact that the history of religious orders shows repeatedly how innovative men and women embraced change and challenge, adapted to new circumstances, and moved the Church forward while keeping her grounded in her traditions.

Chapter 9

OTHER FAITHS

How did the Church relate to other faiths?

The Early Church: Establishing a Separate Identity

When Christianity came on the scene in the Roman Empire, it was considered a strange and confusing movement. Some Jews wondered whether Christianity was a branch of their faith or something entirely new. It sounds odd to our ears, but Romans considered Christians to be Jews or "pagans" because they did not follow the established polytheism of many Roman gods and goddesses. The Romans' multiple ways of worshipping were closely tied to their political and social systems. They saw Jews and Christians as enemies of the state, traitors, outsiders, "pagans," or even "atheists."

Christianity's first task, therefore, was to establish itself as something different: not Jewish, not pagan, not polytheistic, not atheistic. This task had several goals. First, Christians had to explain how belief in Jesus as Savior did not make a believer a different type of Jew, but a follower of a new faith. Second, Christians needed to demonstrate that they were not enemies of Rome, though they were periodically persecuted for nearly 300 years. Third, they had to spell out just what their beliefs were—and these were hard to grasp. How could God be three persons but one God? How could Jesus have died but be alive? How can bread and wine become something else? And just what were those Christians doing in underground meeting places, like the catacombs, and late at night in people's houses? What about the rumors of eating flesh and having orgies?

A group of Christians—called the apologists—set out to explain Christianity to non-Christians. They did not "apologize" as we understand the term today—no one need apologize for being a Christian or a follower of any religion—but the word "apologist" means one who explains and defends. They used emerging creeds, liturgical celebrations, and the writings called Gospels and letters to explain Christians' beliefs and actions. Fundamentally, Romans focused on this world while Christians looked to the next, which put Christians out of step with the society they lived in. So apologists had to dance delicately to explain what Christians believed, but also to convince Romans why Christians should not be considered dangerous because of those beliefs.

Apologists tended to be well-educated Roman citizens who, once converted to Christianity, used their training in Greek and Roman philosophy to explain Christianity in ways that the pagan Romans could understand. They tried to persuade the pagans that Christianity was substantive and not trendy, that Christians were good citizens and not subversive members of a cult, and that the Christian message was open to all and was not a small group of mysterious, dangerous, and untrustworthy rebels.

Apologists took different approaches in explaining Christianity to the Roman and Greek pagans. Justin (later called Justin Martyr), for instance, was a pagan convert to Christianity who had never been a Jew. Born in Palestine about 100 into a wealthy pagan Greek family, he found that Greek philosophy failed to satisfy him fully. After his conversion, he traveled to

Rome, established a school of apologetics there, and wrote several apologies that had a distinctly dispassionate tone. One of his major points was that the soul could not attain direct communion with God without the Holy Spirit. But Justin was not a cold academic: a true believer who did not run from persecution, in 165 he was beheaded for the faith.

Another apologetical document, the anonymous *Letter to Diognetus* from about the year 150, has a more approachable and catechetical style. The author explained that while pagans worshipped God's creations, such as idols made of wood or stone, Christians worshipped God. Christianity, this author went on, fulfills Judaism while avoiding the many rules that had bogged some Jews down, as Jesus himself had said to the Pharisees. This letter stressed Christianity's fundamental monotheism, which was out of step with Roman polytheism. But it also pointed out that Christians and Romans had common ground in ethical values, such as the virtues, stability, and peace on which the *Pax Romana* was built. Another apologist, Athenagoras, wrote a letter explaining Christianity to the Roman emperor about 175–180. He countered the popular charges against Christians: that they engaged in incest, cannibalism, and were subversive "atheists" because they did not believe in the Roman gods. He said that Christianity did not compete with Greco-Roman philosophy and values, but harmonized with them.

Several apologists wrote so much philosophy that the appeal to the intellect left some curious Romans cold or unconvinced. At the same time, Christianity's increasing appeal to artisans, the poor, women, and slaves threatened Romans. The apologists' job became increasingly critical when Roman sentiment hardened against the Christians, who would literally die rather than become pagans.

Because Romans had some experience with Jews, the apologists sometimes started with the Old Testament. They showed how the prophets foretold the Jesus of the New Testament and demonstrated that the God of the Old Testament was the Father of Jesus. Authoritative Christian beliefs came from Scripture and the apostles. This made Christianity less frightening than something entirely new with no past, although the apologists emphasized not only the Jewish roots, but the Christian innovations, too.

A negative side of this, however, began during the first decades of Christianity when believers and leaders (and later writers throughout Church history) tried too hard to distinguish Christianity from Judaism and ended up denigrating Jews. Proponents of this negative attitude appealed to Paul, although they misunderstood what Paul was trying to say in those very first years of Christianity. Recent scholarship seems to have reached a consensus that, in Galatians, Paul was not against Judaism itself or the Jews themselves, but against "agitators" who were insisting that Gentile converts follow Jewish law. Paul saw these agitators as confusing and even dangerous to the new faith, and advocated that they be expelled from the synagogue. For Paul, the main issue was in establishing the particular identity of those who believed that Jesus was the Son of God and the Savior. He was stressing that one need not be a Jew in order to be a Christian. Later in Church history, Paul's goal was misread to say that Paul condemned all Jews. We also find, dating to this early period, words that stand out for their low opinion, even hostility, toward Jews. The *Letter to Diognetus,* written about a hundred years later in the middle of the second century, refers to the Jews as wrong, foolish, and superstitious. Augustine (354–430) noted that Jews give witness to the Old Testament prophecies of Christ, although he identified them with Cain, who killed Abel. John Chrysostom (ca. 347–407) referred to Jews as "degenerate, inebriate dogs" and said that any Christian fraternizing with Jews or failing to block such fellowship is an "enemy of God."

As Christianity moved out of her first stage of development in the early Church, two features should be noted. First, the two strands of attitudes toward Jews would continue to develop, though unfortunately the negative strand would get stronger. Second, Christianity had moved from being a persecuted to a favored religion. So her efforts at evangelization came no longer from an inferior position, but from the most central place in society. This change in status would influence how Christians related to other faiths in the rest of the first millennium.

The First Millennium Church: Converting Pagans

THE PRIMARY QUESTION THAT THE Church faced from about 500 to 1000 was inculturation. How could

Christianity best spread the Gospel message to heretics, such as Arians, who held that Jesus was not fully God, and pagans, who continued to practice the polytheism of the fallen Roman Empire? Most of the action took place in central Europe and the British Isles, where the Church had to relate to other faiths in a way that would teach them the truths of Jesus, Church doctrine, and liturgical practice, but not alienate and prevent them from embracing Christianity.

The practical challenge came down to this: missionaries assimilated pagan rituals, sites, and holy people without sacrificing the essence of Christianity. Otherwise, what resulted would not be new Christians but, at best, Christianized pagans. This strategy came largely from Pope Gregory the Great (590–606), who was intensely interested in spreading the faith. In an influential letter that he sent to a French abbot, Mellitus, who was on his way to England in 601, Gregory advised a soft and pragmatic approach:

> ...[T]he temples of idols in that nation should not be destroyed, but...the idols themselves that are in them should be. Let blessed water be prepared and sprinkled in these temples and altars constructed and relics deposited since, if these same temples are well built, it is needful that they should be transferred from the worship of idols to the service of the true God; that, when the people themselves see that these temples are not destroyed, they may put away error from their heart and, knowing and adoring the true God, may have recourse with the more familiarity to the places they have been accustomed to....[1]

How did this strategy play out? Missionaries found in the pagans a predisposition to faith in the supernatural that made their jobs easier: these people were not atheists, but religious believers already, although they did not believe in Jesus. They tried to channel the pagans' innate religious enthusiasm and their sense of wonder, awe, fear, and respect into Christianity. Some of the most interesting places where this happened were Visigothic Spain, Merovingian and Carolingian Gaul (France), and Anglo-Saxon England in the seventh through the ninth centuries.

Missionaries did not replace the pagans' religious objects and actions, but assigned a greater source or person to them. While pagans might pay more attention to an action (such as a physical cure) or the person performing the action (a *magus* or *medicus*), missionaries identified these cures as miracles. They assigned them to God acting through saints, who were not curing for money as did pagan ministers. Restoring health, therefore, remained a special mark—not of magic, however, but of holiness. This might strike us as superstitious, but in the first millennium, the Church permitted the idea that bells blessed by a holy person (a priest, bishop, abbot, or hermit) could dispel fever or thunder if rung in the right circumstances. It was also common to believe that dust from a saint's tomb, when sprinkled on the eyes of a blind person, could restore sight.

There are other examples of the Church relating positively to other faiths by Christianizing pagan rituals. The Church condemned prophecy or soothsaying by reading an animal's entrails, the flight of birds, or the path of the stars. But missionaries allowed people to believe in angels and demons, the power of relics, and that God could speak to believers in dreams. Christians could not worship nature or believe in astrology, but they could learn from the moon's waxing and waning the moral lesson that every life has good times and bad. Wood was not holy in itself, but the wood of the cross was an instrument of salvation. The most spectacular example would be the alleged "amulet of Charlemagne": two crystal hemispheres bound with gold and worn on a chain around the neck, with what was believed to be a bit of the true cross and a strand of the Blessed Virgin Mary's hair. In this way, the pagan reverence for wood and hair was transferred to a Christian relic.

During the first millennium, Christianity also continued to relate to Jews, picking up on the two strands of attitudes from the early Church. Pope Gregory the Great stated that Jews had certain rights that should not be breached, but that they should recognize their inferiority in relation to Christianity. Later in the period, Pope Stephen IV (768–772) referred to Jews as "sons of darkness."

These centuries also saw Christianity relating to a new faith. Islam came on the scene with Muhammad (ca. 570–632), who wrote his revelations down in the Koran and spread Islam through present-day Saudi Arabia. After his death, Islam expanded rapidly in just one century. Muslims took control of the Holy Land, moved westward across North Africa, turned up on the Iberian Peninsula (today's Spain and Portugal), and crossed the Pyrenees. It expanded there until 732, when

Charlemagne's grandfather Charles Martel turned the
Muslims back. The Mediterranean Sea, for centuries
called a Roman lake, was now Muhammad's lake.
Christianity was now cut off from its Greek, eastern
borders. How Muslims, Christians, and Jews interacted
in the aftermath of this spectacular spread is a story better told from the vantage point of the Middle Ages and
the Crusades.

The Medieval Church: The Crusades

AFTER ISLAM'S APPEARANCE AND RAPID diffusion in the
600s and early 700s, Christians had then lived under
Muslim rule quite peaceably. Like the Jews, Christians
were protected minorities in lands controlled by Islam.
Both Christians and Jews paid a tribute tax, but were
largely left alone to practice their faith and live their
lives. While Christian pilgrims to the Holy Land were
sometimes harassed, assaulted, and even killed during
the Middle Ages, Muslims did not want to stem the
tide of pilgrims. They earned income by allowing
Christians to visit the Church of the Holy Sepulchre in
Jerusalem and the other holy sites in Bethlehem,
Nazareth, Bethany, and elsewhere. This status was different than the state of affairs under Christian rule: on the
whole, it was harder for Jews and Muslims to live, worship, and work freely in Christian countries.

For some persons, a basic understanding of the
other's faith led to some respect and understanding.
Muslims revere Jesus and Mary, although Islam does not
recognize Jesus as the Son of God and the Messiah.

Jesus is a great prophet, second only to Muhammad, in Islam. Informed Muslims saw Christianity as a revelation of God, but not the full revelation represented by Islam. Both were people of law and justice; they agreed on God as the creator of the universe; and some Christians and Muslims understood their shared heritage concerning Abraham and the one God. But Muslims could not understand how God could be one and three at the same time, which made the concept of the Trinity completely alien to them. Sometimes they recorded crusader oaths taken "in the name of the Father, the Son, and the Holy Spirit" as "by God, by God, by God." Nor could some understand how God could be born of a woman, live as a child, and die. Culturally, Muslims saw Christians as inferior, and the same was true the other way around, but each side often praised the other for their skill as warriors. Both Latin and Arabic chronicles frequently demonstrated this, even as they stereotypically said "God (or Allah) damn them!" or used caricature phrases like "dark-skinned" or "blue-eyed." Yet their shared faith in one God did not translate into peaceful relations, while Christians also continued to be largely hostile to Jews.

By the time of the First Crusade (1096–1099), the cultural groundwork had been laid for large-scale Christian violence against the Jews. Medieval Jews were sometimes accused of cheating Christian businessmen, desecrating consecrated hosts, holding "black" masses with the devil, and slaughtering Christian children, especially around Passover, so they could make matzo with the blood. Jews were outsiders in Christian Europe: they could not be guild members, hold land, or be town officials because of the Christian oaths involved. Specifically, there was a dangerous precedent linking Jews, Christians, Muslims, and the Holy Land about a century before the First Crusade. In 1009, a caliph named Hakim ordered the destruction by fire of the Church of the Holy Sepulchre. A group of French Christians claimed the Jews in their local area had put the Muslim Hakim up to it and had even paid him, which led to the mass forced Baptism and slaughter of these Jews.

As the Christians traveled to fight the Muslims in the Holy Land, they waged two sets of major attacks on the Jews. The first set of pogroms followed the calling of the First Crusade in 1095, and the second was related to the Second Crusade in 1146. As the first crusaders left, some asked themselves why they were traveling so far to attack the "infidel" Muslims when the "infidel" Jews were right next door. Pogroms occurred in the spring of 1096, very soon after Pope Urban II called for the Crusade in 1095, in Speyer, Mainz, Cologne, other towns along the Moselle valley, Prague, and Ratisbon. The scenes were repeated in the spring of 1146 in connection with the Second Crusade, with most of the violence occurring in towns and villages in the Rhineland. The violence was extreme, with some Jews choosing to commit suicide rather than give themselves up to forced conversion or death.

Not all Christians were guilty. A number of bishops sheltered Jews, although some later decided to withdraw their protection. A few put their own lives on the line, faced the crowds calling for Jewish blood, and saved Jewish lives. The Cistercian abbot Bernard of Clairvaux (1090–1153), who preached the Second Crusade on the pope's command, was enraged at the attacks against Jews. He wrote one letter denouncing a monk who claimed to have been sent by God to promote the Crusade and to tell the armies to start with the Jews. In another document, an open letter to the English people, Bernard bluntly wrote: "I have heard with great joy of the zeal for God's glory which burns in your midst, but your zeal needs the timely restraint of knowledge. The Jews are not to be persecuted, killed, or even put to flight." In language that seems like a back-handed endorsement, he said it was better to convert the Jews: "The Jews are for us the living words of Scripture, for they remind us always of what our Lord suffered. They are dispersed all over the world so that by expiating their crime they may be everywhere the living witnesses of our redemption."[2]

After the Crusades, Jews were sometimes converted forcibly, as in Spain in the thirteenth century, and periodically expelled from countries, such as England in 1290, France in 1306, and Spain in 1492. Some popes tried to offer a measure of safety for the Jews, especially against forced Baptism and the "blood libel." This was the intent of Pope Innocent III in 1199 and Pope Gregory X in 1272, although the Fourth Lateran Council in 1215 mandated that Jews wear distinctive clothing to identify themselves.

Here, then, are examples that can be interpreted in a positive and negative light, especially with the 20/20 hindsight of the modern reader. It reminds us that

Jewish-Christian-Muslim relations, especially with respect to the Crusades, are complex relationships, indeed.

The Reformation Church:
A Divided Christianity Spreads

AS WE MOVE INTO THE FIFTEENTH century and beyond, the story of how the Church related to other faiths changes dramatically for two reasons. First, the known world expanded in the age of exploration. This brought new opportunities to spread the faith to people who were not monotheists and who had no connection to European civilization. Second, the Reformation shattered the Church's unity, dividing Catholic and Protestant Christians. Protestantism itself was sub-divided into a number of denominations: Lutherans, Calvinists, Anglicans, Anabaptists, Methodists, etc.

Before Columbus crossed the Atlantic in 1492, European explorers had been making their way to the Far East. They sailed around the tip of Africa and traveled along land routes, too. Along with exploration came evangelization of people who had never heard of Jesus. Catholics at the time would have called them pagans, albeit of a different variety than the ones Christianity encountered in the first millennium.

European monarchs saw it as their royal duty to sponsor missionaries. The popes happily gave kings and queens a fairly free rein, since they were paying for and physically protecting the missions. In 1508, Pope Julius II (1503–1513) even granted Spain's Ferdinand and Isabella ecclesiastical rights in mission territories: the monarchs paid the clergy, established dioceses, built churches, and named bishops. Encounters, however, often became violent; the indigenous populations of the Americas were told to become Christians or face slavery or death. Mass Baptisms in the Americas and in India raised the question of how Christian these converts really were. Soon, provincial councils in sixteenth-century Peru warned against quick Baptisms, emphasizing catechesis instead.

Explorers motivated by "God, glory, and gold!" often simply wiped out whatever native faith was in their way. This happened in Hernando Cortés' 1519 to 1521 massacre of the Aztecs in modern-day Mexico, and Francisco Pizarro's conquest of the Incas in Peru that same century. When Ferdinand Magellan arrived in 1521 in the Philippines, he set up a large cross for Easter Sunday and made all the native leaders venerate it. One village that refused was burned to the ground, causing the battle in which Magellan was himself killed. North American missionaries regularly referred to the indigenous populations around the Great Lakes in modern-day Canada and the United States as "savages."

Some missionaries, perhaps unconsciously building on the first millennium methods of Pope Gregory the Great, learned native languages for their catechesis classes. Baptism, Confession, and Marriage were freely offered, though Holy Communion and sometimes ordination were withheld. Most famously, the Jesuits realized that to succeed in China and Japan, they had to adapt to the culture. They dressed as wise men and accommodated Christianity to Asian ideas instead of imposing Europe's foreign Latin culture. The Jesuit Matteo Ricci (1552–1610) entered China dressed as a Buddhist monk, learned Chinese, studied Confucius, dressed as a scholar, and finally converted members of the imperial court to Christianity. (This effort led to the Chinese Rites Controversy, which we will explore in the early modern period, when the conflict was strongest.) Jesuits in what became Brazil and Canada learned the local languages and customs, taught catechesis, and only baptized after sufficient instruction.

In 1568, Pope Pius V instituted the Congregation of Cardinals for the Conversion of Infidels (whose last word certainly places the action in its historical context). In 1622, the papacy established the Congregation for the Propagation of the Faith, which subsumed a number of Roman departments and earlier efforts concerned with the missions. The popes wanted to regulate monarchs, who thought they should control Christianity in the new territories as they had essentially done for about a century. The Roman concern may sound surprisingly forward-thinking: the Church wanted missionaries not to impose a European Christianity and clergy (which was the royal method), but to let an indigenous Christianity with a local clergy emerge as soon as possible.

The second major way the Church related to other faiths in this period concerned the conflict that arose when Christianity split: Catholics on one side and several Protestant denominations on the other. We must remember, however, that much of what happened from about 1520 to 1648 had as much to do with political and military power as with religious belief. After Luther posted his *Ninety-Five Theses* in 1517 and the Protestant revolution ensued, things didn't settle down until the *Peace of Augsburg* in 1555. That agreement allowed rulers to choose either Catholicism or Lutheranism for their territories. A truce lasted from 1555 until 1618, when the Thirty Years' War broke out between German Catholics and Protestants. The fight spread across Europe with countries lining up into a Protestant Union versus a Catholic League, although infighting occurred even under these two umbrellas. With the *Peace of Westphalia* in 1648, Europe was largely split three ways: Catholics, Lutherans, and Calvinists (called Huguenots in France). This treaty stipulated that a ruler could not impose his religion, but he could regulate public worship while permitting private worship.

Several things happened as a result of all this. First, religion itself suffered and became devalued. It strongly influenced people's lives, to be sure, but it was now just one of several major influences along with social change, political upheaval, and cultural unrest. Second, the Protestant criticisms and the Catholic responses ushered in a period not of ecumenism, but of religious conflict and theological debate—a Christian "cold war." Catholics and Protestants rarely spoke with each other; instead, they yelled at each other. Diatribe replaced what little dialogue had occurred. Polemicists and apologists on both sides of the Christian divide wrote academic treatises and popular essays designed to show why their version of Christianity was right and the others were wrong. Third, and more positively, the missions became a place where Christianity could spread. Catholics at first established missions far more than Protestants did, in large part because Catholicism's central organization facilitated such efforts. Over the centuries, Protestants turned to the missions, too, especially in Africa and Asia during the imperial and colonial periods of the early modern and modern world. There they also faced the interesting challenges of balancing inculturation, assimilation, and accommodation when they encountered polytheistic faiths.

The Early Modern Church: Encountering New Challenges

IN THE PERIOD AFTER THE COUNCIL OF TRENT concluded in 1563, Catholicism looked both within and beyond herself to renew the Church and spread the faith. During this period, the Scientific Revolution and the Enlightenment challenged faith itself. People questioned whether or not religious belief could exist peacefully with rationalism. Faith had already been battered by the Wars of Religion, as we have just seen, and Catholicism did not have good relations with other faiths, especially Protestant denominations. The challenges of this great missionary period—begun right before Trent, but really taking root in the early modern centuries—returned the Church to earlier questions: how to deal with believers who did not share with Catholics a language of monotheism; the theological principles of Trinity, Incarnation, and resurrection; a system of liturgy and sacraments; and a Church structure.

Missionaries took different approaches to converting indigenous populations in the Americas, Asia, and
Africa. While some missionaries, especially in the "New
World" of the Americas, tended to convert from the
bottom of society and move upward, in Asia the effort
was largely to target the top of society and work down-
ward. That reflected what had tended to occur in
northern Europe in the first millennium. In both cases,
the missionaries tried to develop a clergy from the
indigenous population as soon as possible, but continued the general movement of preventing them from
joining religious orders.

Two separate congregations in Rome directed the
missions: the Propagation of the Faith in Africa and the
Propagation of the Faith in Asia. In 1659, a directive
from the office for Asia—reminiscent of the instructions of Pope Gregory I to a missionary on his way to
England over a thousand years before—indicated a
measure of openness to indigenous believers and customs rather than a heavy-handed approach:

> Do not demand of those peoples that they change
> their ceremonies, customs, and habits if these do not
> quite obviously contradict religion and decency, for
> what could be sillier than to want to import France,
> Spain, Italy, or any other country into China? Not
> these but the faith is what you shall bring to them,
> which neither rejects nor fights against any peoples'
> customs and traditions, but rather seeks to keep them
> inviolate.[3]

Meanwhile, in the "New World" of the Americas,
the Franciscans generally took a fairly strong, even mil-

itaristic approach, that sometimes forced Christianity onto people. The Franciscans were not the only religious order who could be heavy-handed: history records that religious orders including the Jesuits held slaves in Central and South America as well as in the southern United States. Others were, in one way or another, connected with the slave trade at its source in Africa. Their efforts to evangelize were tangled and slowed by tribal warfare, European slave traders who were spreading through Africa along with missionaries, and frequent reversals of fortune.

Some missionaries may have taken a strong, even violent approach, because of the fear or danger of syncretism, whereby Christianity would take on so many indigenous beliefs and practices that the faith lost its essentials and stopped being authentic Christianity. This concern led the archbishop of Lima in Peru to order "idolatry inspections" in 1640. A strict hand could be used to ward syncretism off, which led one eighteenth-century Mayan to remark that he hoped Christ would appear in his second coming—so he would throw out the Spanish and restore the Mayan kingdoms and social structures.

An effective way to examine this question is to take a case-study approach by looking specifically at the Jesuit missions in Asia and, especially, the Chinese Rites Controversy referred to previously. While it is sometimes hard to pin down precisely what the Chinese Rites were, it appears that they included some ceremonies honoring the philosopher Confucius, ancestor worship, and the adoption of Chinese ideas approximating heaven and an omniscient God that seemed close enough to Christian concepts. The Jesuit missionaries in China also tapped into a Chinese philosophy that was predisposed to monotheism, emphasized a concept of ethics rather than a list of sins, and only rarely displayed a crucifix, since the symbol of a dead God (as some put it) puzzled the Chinese. This set the stage, therefore, to slip into syncretism if the Jesuits were not careful and went too far down the road of accommodation.

How did Rome respond? With mixed signals. Early in the seventeenth century, Pope Paul V (1605–1621) approved the saying of Mass in Chinese, while in 1603 a Jesuit official had allowed ancestor worship and the ceremonies for Confucius. In 1645, Rome condemned ancestor worship, but in 1656, Pope Alexander VII approved the Jesuit strategy. From 1705 to 1715, some European monarchs who were bankrolling the Jesuit missions backed their approach, but about the same time Pope Clement XI reasserted the condemnation of ancestor worship. In 1745, Pope Benedict XIV finally prohibited the Chinese Rites.

In various places and at different times, then, the Catholic Church related to people of other faiths, especially in the missions, with diverse approaches and therefore with mixed results. The temptation to accommodate often arose, but the need for inculturating the faith was also crucial. In nearly every case, however, Catholicism's general approach was one of dominance. In the modern period, however, the perspective and emphasis would shift.

The Modern Church: A New Openness

VATICAN II (1962–1965) BUILT ON decades of very slow and careful steps to change the way Catholicism related to people of other faiths. So much changed at Vatican II and in its aftermath that we must focus on the council to pursue this most recent chapter in this story.

In its document on missionary activity, *Ad Gentes* (1965), the Council noted specifically that the opportunity to expand the faith in diverse cultures requires a variety of perspectives and approaches as well as a respect for local custom. *Ad Gentes* specifically prohibited forced conversions and repeated the Church's longstanding policy of promoting an indigenous clergy. The document on ecumenism, *Unitatis Redintegratio* (1964), viewed the past history of Protestants and Catholics with frankness and sadness, but hoped for a better future. It recognized that there was plenty of blame to go around, but instructed Catholics to go in a different direction. It urged them to engage Protestants in dialogue in a spirit of respect and learning, never forgetting their common bond in Jesus. Since then, great progress—though not without significant stumbles—has taken place as people of many Christian faiths (Orthodox, Anglican, Lutheran, etc.) have tried to move closer together by studying key theological concepts, human institutions, and historical developments.

For our story, we should take special care to look back to the medieval heritage among Jews, Muslims, and Christians to see the change brought about by Vatican II. We begin with the Church and Jewish people. In recent years especially, people have often debated the degree to which the Catholic Church and individual Christians have or have not contributed to a mainstream anti-Semitism that can be found throughout Western history. At the same time, Pope John Paul II particularly tried to improve relations between Jews and Christians, specifically Catholics. On several occasions, he referred with great respect to the Jews as the Christians' elder brothers and sisters. He also apologized for the violence against the Jews that was a terrible part of Church history. In March 2000, he visited Israel, prayed at *Yad Vashem* (Israel's Holocaust memorial and museum), and left a note in the Western Wall asking forgiveness for the sins committed by members of the Church against Jews throughout history.

Indeed, the idea that all Jews—past, present, and future—were guilty of Jesus' murder was a standard belief changed only explicitly when Vatican II issued *Nostra Aetate* (1965):

> Although the Jewish authorities with their followers pressed for the death of Christ, still those things which were perpetuated during his passion cannot be ascribed indiscriminately to all the Jews living at the time nor to the Jews of today. Although the Church is the new people of God, the Jews should not be represented as rejected by God or accursed…. [The Church] deplores feelings of hatred, persecutions, and demonstrations of anti-Semitism directed against the Jews at whatever time and by whomsoever. (no. 4)

In practical terms, some Catholics may recall a pre-Vatican II liturgical reference to the "perfidious Jews."

But now, during the Good Friday liturgy, Catholics pray respectfully for the Jewish people as the first to hear the voice of God.

The Church has also sought to improve her official relations with Muslims, starting with a statement found in a document Pope Paul VI issued in 1964 titled *Ecclesiam Suam* (1964):

> Then [we refer] to the adorers of God according to the conception of monotheism, the Muslim religion especially, deserving of our admiration for all that is true and good in their worship of God." (no. 107)

That same year, Vatican II also addressed the Muslims in *Lumen Gentium:*

> But the plan of salvation also includes those who acknowledge the Creator, in the first place among whom are the Muslims: these profess to hold the faith of Abraham, and together with us they adore the one, merciful God, mankind's judge on the last day." (no. 16)

The council's most extensive comments came in *Nostra Aetate,* which also singled out positive links with Hinduism and Buddhism:

> The Church has also a high regard for the Muslims. They worship God, who is one, living and subsistent, merciful and almighty, the Creator of heaven and earth, who has spoken to men. [Muslims] strive to submit themselves without reserve to the hidden decrees of God, just as Abraham submitted himself to God's plan, to whose faith Muslims eagerly linked their own. Although not acknowledging him as God, they venerate Jesus as a prophet, his Virgin Mother

they also honor, and even at times devoutly invoke. Further, they await the day of judgment and the reward of God following the resurrection of the dead. For this reason they highly esteem an upright life and worship God, especially by way of prayer, alms-deeds, and fasting.

Over the centuries many quarrels and dissensions have arisen between Christians and Muslims. The sacred Council [Vatican II] now pleads with all to forget the past, and urges that a sincere effort be made to achieve mutual understanding; for the benefit of all men, let them together preserve and promote peace, social justice and moral values. (no. 3)

Progress is being made. In October 1999, an interreligious assembly met in Rome and agreed on several joint statements, including the following:

We are all aware that interreligious collaboration does not imply giving up our own religious identity but is rather a journey of discovery. We learn to respect one another as members of the one human family. We learn to appreciate both our differences and the common values that bind us to one another.... As we study the history of other religious traditions as well as of our own, we confess that much has gone wrong in the past. We must recognize and acknowledge these wrongs, express our sorrow about them and condemn what deserves condemnation. We commit ourselves to try to do everything in our power so that such actions or omissions not be repeated. Such steps can foster a process of understanding and reconciliation.[4]

We should return to Pope John Paul II, since he did so much to improve relations between Catholics and people of other faiths. In his statement on the third millennium, *Novo Millennio Ineunte* (2001), he said:

> It is in this context (of openness to God's grace) also that we should consider the great challenge to interreligious dialogue to which we shall still be committed in the new millennium, in fidelity to the teachings of the Second Vatican Council....This dialogue must continue. In the climate of increased cultural and religious pluralism which is expected to mark the society of the new millennium, it is obvious that this dialogue will be especially important in establishing a sure basis for peace and [for] warding off the dread specter of those wars of religion which have so often bloodied human history. The name of the one God must become increasingly what it is: a name of peace and a summons to peace. (no. 55)

The times, indeed, have changed.

Chapter 10

GREATEST CHALLENGES

What were the greatest challenges the Church has ever faced?

The Early Church: Fighting for Her Life

THE FIRST CHALLENGE THE CHURCH FACED was to establish her identity and fight for her survival. Were Christians Jews—and did you have to be a Jew to be a Christian? Were Christians traitors to the Roman Empire because they were "pagans" and "atheists" to the Roman gods? These were essential questions that the new Christians had to settle for themselves. Then they had to effectively communicate their answers to non-Christians, especially Roman officials.

The first question, of course, was to determine the relationship of Jews to the followers of Jesus. "Jewish-Christians," like the apostles and Mary, believed Jesus was the Messiah, which separated them from Jews who did not share their belief. These Jesus-following Jews were also worshipping together, often in synagogues, and living with a foot in both worlds of belief. Peter and Paul both began to reach out to non-Jews, indicating that one didn't have to be Jewish to follow Jesus. Peter ate with Cornelius, for example, while Paul, Timothy, and Barnabas branched out to Gentiles almost exclusively. In Jerusalem, the Jews who followed Jesus were called Nazarenes, to denote that they followed Jesus of Nazareth. But in Antioch, where a good-sized group of Jesus' followers emerged, they were called *Christianoi*—men of Christ.

The question came to a head in A.D. 49 or 50 at a gathering that is known as the Council of Jerusalem (although it is not listed as one of the Church's twenty-one ecumenical councils). There, Peter, Paul, James, and other leaders agreed that a Christian need not be a Jew, but that those who followed Jesus should adhere to Jewish laws on diet and sexual behavior. Still, Jews and Christians continued to compete for converts, with the "Jesus community" of Jews moving further away from Judaism and the Gentile Christians growing rapidly. The admonition to hold onto Mosaic Law fell away and so, by about 100, Christianity and Judaism had effectively separated. This allowed Christianity's religious identity, at least with respect to Judaism, to be fairly clear.

The second question of identity did not deal with the Jewish-Christian community, but concerned how Christians dealt with the pagan Roman culture in which they lived precariously. This question, however, was linked a bit with Judaism, since Jews had a tenuous relationship with Rome. In A.D. 40, the mad Roman emperor Caligula ordered that a statue of himself as a god be set up in Jerusalem's Temple. Although he was assassinated before this could occur, Caligula's order increased tensions, and a few years later Peter was arrested in Jerusalem. He escaped and began the journey that would bring him to Rome.

Rome had a polytheistic, pagan culture, but Roman officials like the emperor Tiberius periodically moved to suppress "foreign" religions. They feared that non-Roman "cults"—Egypt's Isis, Judaism's Yahweh, or Christianity's Jesus—would pull Romans away from loyalty to the state. To be a Roman citizen meant that you believed in Rome's many pagan gods and in the idea that a Roman emperor could become a god. After the emperor Augustus' death in A.D. 14, for example, he was proclaimed a god. His successor Tiberius banned all non-Roman religious activities, liturgical celebrations, objects, and vestments. The state judged Christians in Rome, then, as subversive: a Christian was a traitor to Rome and threatened the safety and security of the empire.

Christians had to fight for their lives, but persecution was not constant. It came, rather, in waves of relative toleration and attack. Nero, the Roman emperor who fiddled while Rome burned, blamed the infamous city fire of A.D. 64 on the Christians and ordered them killed in large numbers. Some were tied to posts and were burned alive as human torches that Nero strolled past in his gardens. Both Peter and Paul were martyred during this round of persecutions.

Relative toleration followed in the latter part of the first century and early half of the second. Christians were generally left alone and not hunted out. If captured, they were given several chances to recant and were not always punished with death. In a famous letter of instruction, the emperor Trajan told the provincial governor Pliny that Christians could not be denounced anonymously or convicted without hard evidence. By the end of the second century, Christianity was flourishing not only in the city of Rome, but throughout the provinces of the empire. The new faith was formidable; it attracted more slaves, artisans, women, and children who practiced their beliefs with rising fervor. The danger of subversion grew as the empire began its long, slow implosion. Provincial governors, eager to demonstrate their ability to maintain order and loyalty, began to change strategies. They sought Christians out to find the "atheists" who followed a foreign, alien god. They encouraged mob violence, spying, and public denouncements. Local attacks followed, which quickly increased the ranks of martyrs.

By A.D. 193, Christianity was one of the larger religions of the ancient world, with a more organized network of affiliation than other religions. This made it a shadow organization that competed with Rome. By A.D. 201, converting to Judaism or Christianity was made a capital crime. Wide-scale, systematic persecutions followed in A.D. 250 to 260 under the emperors Decius and Valerian. Both of them stood on their role as chief priest (*pontifex maximus*) to defend Rome from the "pagan" Christians, who were charged with conspiracy, treason, atheism, and unlawful assembly. The worst persecution followed half a century later under Diocletian in A.D. 303 to 305. Roman authority was collapsing at this time, and Diocletian laid the blame on the faithlessness and atheism of anyone who did not follow Roman paganism and polytheism. He dismissed Christians from public service, destroyed church buildings, confiscated Scripture and liturgical vessels, and deprived aristocratic Christians of their social status.

Perhaps the best way to demonstrate how Christianity turned the ideas of atheism and paganism around is to recount the story of Polycarp, the bishop of Smyrna in modern Turkey in the middle of the second century. Nearing 90, Polycarp was arrested and brought before the Roman provincial governor. He ordered Polycarp to recant his belief in Christ and say, "Away with the atheists!"—meaning the Christians whom he led as bishop. Polycarp responded by saying, "Away with the atheists!" as he pointed not to the Christians who were there, but to the Romans who had turned out to see his trial. The Christians had forged a clear identity.

The First Millennium Church: Spreading the Faith

CHRISTIANITY SOON MOVED FROM being persecuted to being the only game in the Roman towns. The emperor Constantine officially tolerated and protected Christianity in 313, and the emperor Theodosius made Christianity the only legal religion in the empire in 380. As a result, Christianity had to reverse gears and bring pagans—now meaning non-Christians—into its own fold, especially in central and northern Europe. After Islam spread rapidly across the Mideast, North Africa, and Spain from 632 to 732, Christianity looked north to expand. There, Christian missionaries discovered pagans who already believed in the supernatural, even if they did not believe in one God or in the concept of the Son of God.

In northern Europe, Christians found a mixture of confused Christianity, leftover pieces of Roman paganism, and remnants of indigenous polytheism. These were often mixed in some very strange combinations that had formed as the Roman Empire withered and withdrew from its farthest borders. The challenge was to untangle all of it while not alienating potential believers. At the same time, an authentic Christianity had to be taught and sustained so that, in the end, Europe did not hold a Christianized paganism, but true Christianity in belief and practice. Missionaries found a solution: not to impose Christianity harshly, but to introduce it gradually with sensitivity and tolerance. While that might not be the textbook caricature of how Christianity spread—and this is not to deny the brutality of some of the Spanish Inquisition's actions in the medieval and early modern periods—it is largely the truer story in the first millennium.

The Church took on the task of evangelization. By the end of the first millennium, Christianity had done well. The faith had reached Poland by 966, Hungary a few years later, and Russia by 988. The Church also was leaving the door open: in 968, for example, the archdiocese of Magdeburg was set up, but without a border on the eastern front. Meanwhile, across the English Channel, Christianity had been spreading up the British Isles and Ireland since Patrick and Augustine of Canterbury had begun their missionary work in the fifth and sixth centuries. There, they decided not so much to impose Christianity as to incorporate existing elements of Anglo-Saxon and Celtic culture into the practice of the faith. Thus, designs such as circles, braids, and knots worked their way into liturgical vestments, altar cloths, linens, and illuminated manuscripts.

Even sacrifice was permitted, within parameters. As Pope Gregory the Great (590–606) had advised missionaries to the north:

Nor let them any longer sacrifice animals to the devil, but [it is permissible to let them] slay animals to the praise of God for their own eating, and return thanks to the Giver of all.... For it is undoubtedly impossible to cut away everything at once from hard hearts, since one who strives to ascend to the highest place must needs rise by steps or paces, and not by leaps.[1]

An example—disturbing, but instructive nevertheless—of how this worked in practice comes from Scandinavia in the 1070s where, in Uppsala, a chronicler reported that he witnessed seventy-two dogs, horses, and human beings hanged for sacrifice. Similarly, Christianity came to Iceland in 999, where the leaders accepted Baptism, but at the same time the bishops allowed them to continue the practice of infanticide by leaving unwanted newborns out in the cold and exposed to animals.

Other, more benevolent examples make the point. Tapping into local beliefs that a natural spring was a sacred, if pagan, place, Christian missionaries set up baptismal fonts at those sites where people were already going for spiritual rituals. Pagan farmers had typically sprinkled their fields with blood or water to encourage the soil to be fruitful. Adapting this practice, missionary priests and monks in Germany mixed soil from the field with oil, honey, milk, tree bark, and herbs. Then they formed the mixture into clods, laid them on an altar, said Mass, and prayed: "Grow and multiply and replenish the earth."

Then, as now, the Sign of the Cross was a powerful symbol and action, even if it was used more as a talisman than anything else. If a soldier was bleeding on the battlefield, it was believed that making the Sign of the Cross over the wound could stop the blood flow. When two roads came together at intersections—"cross-roads"—this became a logical place to erect a small shrine where a traveler might pray for continued safety on the journey. The Eucharist, of course, was most powerful of all and was sometimes worn around the neck as protection on a trip or during a war.

Was the challenge of bringing the people from paganism to Christianity with this soft approach successful? The answer, alas, must be: not always. We have a report of an Anglo-Saxon priest from this period who didn't know the Old Testament from the New Testament. We also know that some priests baptized "In the name of the fatherland, the daughter, and the Holy Spirit." Bishops repeatedly banned Christians from worshipping natural objects like trees and rocks. In the Nordic countries, only gradually did Jesus emerge as dominant among the pantheon of Norse gods. These examples, however, seem to stand out as the humorous exceptions and not the rule of effective evangelization efforts.

Despite the best efforts of missionaries, however, Christianity and paganism still coexisted in a muddle sometimes, as an early eleventh-century confession manual indicates. Bishop Burchard of Worms' book, the *Corrector,* listed sins and their corresponding penances around the end of this period. Two years of fasting on certain days was the penance for someone who admitted she asked a magician for help to find something that she had lost, to predict the future, or to ask for rain for the family fields. It was a sin to dance or drink on a grave, to seek a woman's help in making a love potion, or to consult the stars for advice on when to fight a war, to marry, to plant, or to start building a house. One striking question Burchard laid down was to ask penitents whether they had put their children on their roofs or in their ovens in order to cure them of a sickness. If the parent had, the confessor put the mother or father on three weeks of bread and water.

Authentic Christianity, it appears, at certain times and in certain places still had far to go. As the Middle Ages approached, a paganized Christianity or a Christianized paganism still existed in some places in Europe. Nevertheless, Christianity had indeed spread far in the millennium after Jesus' resurrection. If the Church continued to contend with beliefs and practices that required monitoring and correction, she still had a system of beliefs, practices, and ministers as a touchstone for the second millennium.

The Medieval Church: Three Popes at Once

Perhaps the darkest moment in the history of the Church, and certainly one of her greatest challenges ever, occurred in a nearly forty-year span in the late fourteenth and early fifteenth centuries. At that time two, and then three, popes claimed to be the true successor to St. Peter. This period from 1378 to 1417 is known as the Great Western Schism. It should not be confused with the schism between East and West that lasted officially from 1054 to 1965.

The Great Western Schism began shortly after the papacy returned from its long stay in Avignon in southern France. When Pope Gregory XI returned to Rome in 1377, the people felt great relief and hope because the papacy had returned where it belonged. But when he died a year later, confusion broke out. The College of Cardinals was small, having only twenty-two members. Of these, only sixteen were in Rome and therefore able to take part in the election. Eleven of them were French, and they clearly wanted the papacy to return to Avignon. The Roman people, however, had been without their bishop for seventy-five years, and the Roman economy had suffered because the papal curia had moved away. (Consider what would happen to the economy of Washington, D.C., if the federal government relocated, and you get a notion of how bureaucracy can create local jobs.)

The night before the conclave, representatives of Roman neighborhoods were permitted to raise their concerns to the cardinals, who had witnessed minor riots during Gregory XI's funeral and so already had a sense of the danger. The 1378 conclave split between two French candidates and the impatient Romans began rioting outside the conclave. Fearful for their lives, the cardinals pretended to elect an 80-year-old Italian cardinal, dressed him in papal robes, and sent him out to the crowd.

Meanwhile, the cardinals escaped to the Castel Sant'Angelo down the road where they picked a compromise candidate who was the last non-cardinal ever to be elected pope. Archbishop Bartolomeo Prignano was Neapolitan by birth, but had spent the last fifteen years in the Avignon curia. As Urban VI, he reigned as pope until 1389, but within a few months of his election in the spring of 1378, things turned ugly. Urban probably suffered from some sort of megalomania: he was obstinate, pugnacious, impetuous, and indiscreet. The French cardinals looked down on him because he was from a lower social class and had not been a member of the College of Cardinals. Urban called one cardinal a dimwit and physically assaulted another. He refused to return to Avignon and denounced the cardinals' lavish lifestyles.

The French cardinals fought back. Claiming that the pope was not giving them their due respect, they said that their election of Urban VI had been invalid because it had been made in fear of the Roman mob—even though for several weeks after the election they had attended his coronation, assisted him in papal liturgies, and sent official letters to Europe's rulers announcing the election. By the fall of 1378, they had fled Rome, charged Urban with mental instability, declared the papacy vacant, and elected one of their own as Clement VII.

The split soon deepened. Urban and Clement sent military forces against each other, but the few battles were draws. Clement gained the allegiance of the existing College of Cardinals, which made Urban name new cardinals and excommunicate the others. Clement, of course, returned the excommunications. Finally, Clement VII returned to Avignon, and Europe split its allegiance.

France, Castile, and Scotland backed the Avignon papacy, while northern Italy, England, Germany, Hungary, Aragon, and Portugal backed Rome—but many of the allegiances were as much about political rivalry as they were about religious fidelity.

Each time a Roman or Avingonese pope died, the other side told his College of Cardinals that they must not elect a successor. But each side continued to claim it was legitimate, so both Rome and Avignon had conclaves and elected new popes for several decades. In 1409, cardinals from both sides decided that three decades was enough. They called a council in Pisa to settle the matter, but they made a critical mistake: they deposed both the Roman and Avignon popes, but did not get them to agree to the depositions. So both popes simply ignored the actions and the council's election of a supposedly unifying pope, who of course named his own College of Cardinals, too. This resulted in three popes, three Colleges of Cardinals, and, in some cases, several local bishops or abbots competing for power. Religious orders split along national lines as well. Things were so confusing that, in the Spanish city of Toledo, during the part of the Mass where Catholics pray for the pope and local bishop, the priest said in Latin *pro illo qui est verus papa*—loosely translated, "for the true pope, whichever one he is."

Learning from the failed council of Pisa (which is not one of the Church's twenty-one ecumenical councils), a general council at Constance met in 1414 and over the next four years moved more slowly and carefully. It deposed two popes (the Pisan and the Avignon, although the latter maintained his claim to the papacy with little backing until he died several years later) and allowed the Roman Pope Gregory XII to resign after officially reconvening the council in his name. Gregory XII knew that this would legitimate any subsequent action the council would take. He also knew that Urban VI and the Roman popes who followed had the true claim to the papacy: there had been no provision in canon law that invalidated an election because it had been made in a rush or in fear of violence—which had been the French cardinals' claim almost forty years before.

To make sure that the mistake of Pisa would not be repeated, the conclave was expanded. All three Colleges of Cardinals participated, as did a group of delegates from the council of Constance. Miraculously, the 1417 conclave lasted only a few days. The man they elected— Martin V (1417–1431)—was able to keep the peace. He essentially pardoned all the prior rivals and went out of his way to give jobs to men from all three allegiances in his own curia. In the next few decades, the papacy worked to restore its prestige and win back power from the general councils, but it had been wounded and weakened. The princely Renaissance popes who followed did little to help the pope's religious importance. In fact, they gave much material to the Catholic and Protestant critics who would soon follow.

The Reformation Church: Admitting Problems

IT IS NOT TRUE THAT CATHOLICS WERE blind to their problems until Martin Luther showed up. In fact, Catholics throughout the Middle Ages had been calling for reform in large numbers and loud voices. But too often their criticisms were dismissed or reforms were not put into place systematically. When Martin Luther and the other reformers who eventually broke away from Rome appeared, some of what they said agreed with what Catholics were saying, too. So the challenge arose: how could one remain Catholic and be considered orthodox when some of what one was saying agreed with reformers whom the Church labeled as heretics?

The best example of this dilemma appears in the person of Erasmus. He lived just about the same time as Luther and said many of the same things about pious actions, although they would have serious debates and disagreements on matters of theology. Some said at the time that Erasmus had laid the egg that Luther hatched, implicitly blaming Erasmus for Luther. While some cardinals wanted to condemn Erasmus as a heretic and perhaps even arrest and burn him at the stake, others wanted to acknowledge his wisdom by granting Erasmus a red hat.

Erasmus called for self-honesty, self-critique, and self-reform, but not everyone wanted to hear that message. This was especially true after Luther and the others started to prove, essentially, that Erasmus had been right all along in certain matters, particularly concerning religious practices. For years before Luther, Erasmus had asked readers to read the Gospels for themselves and to identify closely with the person and actions of Jesus as he is encountered in the New Testament. Then, they should take these insights and express the life of Christ in their own daily lives. While this message does not strike Vatican II ears as strange, in his own time some accused Erasmus of ignoring Church procedures and practices. They also said he was paving the way for Luther once he also began to focus on an individual's own relationship with Christ, sometimes to the exclusion of a priest as intermediary or the Church as arbiter of belief and practice.

Today we understand more of this complex Erasmus-Luther situation, and the many other examples it represents, because of a major effort among historians. Over the last fifty years, they have tried to break down the walls between Catholics and Protestants of the fifteenth and sixteenth centuries—in part because of Vatican II's ecumenical efforts of working toward unity. Scholars have found that, in fact, there were more continuities than discontinuities between Catholics and Protestants as well as between the medieval and Reformation centuries. As many cheap shots as clean shots were thrown during those eras. But once the Protestants and Catholics had separated after the 1520s, it became hard, if not impossible and even dangerous, for Catholics (especially in leadership positions at the level of bishop and higher) to admit that some of the Protestant criticisms were fair, justified, and flat-out correct. The trick was how to stay Catholic and not be labeled a closet Protestant, which was akin to consorting with the enemy.

Both Luther and Erasmus, for example, rightly criticized arithmetical piety: for instance, the notion that two Hail Marys was somehow twice as good as one regardless of one's fervor in praying. Too many Christians focused on what they were doing and how many times they were doing it—going to Mass, walking on a pilgrimage, saying a prayer, collecting a relic, stockpiling indulgences, and on and on during this extremely pious age—rather than on why the Church offered these activities. Church leadership, at the same time, could be equally culpable. After all, bishops and alms collectors did not stop gathering the money when people started missing the point, so there is plenty of criticism to go around from the bottom up in the Church as well as from the top down.

But while we live in an era of ecumenism today, people had little incentive to bridge the Catholic-Protestant divide in the Reformation centuries. After Trent, especially, Catholicism responded to the challenge of admitting problems by becoming generally stricter and less tolerant of diversity. But changing circumstances also made the Church less universal, less dominant, and less commanding of a Christian's ultimate loyalty because of both nationalism and new Protestant denominational options. This move or stance is sometimes called the "Counter-Reformation" to emphasize the attempts to fight back against Protestants, but it is not the whole story. Some reformers responded to the challenge by continuing to press for reform, even when it was a bit dangerous to do so. Some of these found their works on the *Index of Forbidden Books* for the next several centuries, even though they were not saying anything unorthodox at all.

Although the Church did attempt to "counter" the Protestants, this should not obscure the long-standing, continuous effort that pre-dated Luther and post-dated

Trent. This effort emphasized personal reform, an activist spirituality, and an authentic faith that was not in any way unorthodox or Protestant theologically. Both before and after Luther and Trent, we can find Catholics attending sermons, going to confession, marching in *Corpus Christi* processions, and attending religious festivals and instructive morality plays. If they were literate, they also kept religious journals and attended what we would today call Bible study groups in private homes.

The lesson of Luther and Trent, and the challenge to which both Protestants and Catholics had to respond, is that a Christian can be both faithful and critical at the same time. In addition, a Christian can simultaneously attend to individual reform and institutional change. The movement to help individuals and institutions met with limited success before Luther and Trent. But the seeds of both self-reform and institutional rejuvenation were sown by people like Erasmus, fanned by people like Luther, and continued by some popes, bishops, and people in the pews after Trent. That council tried to focus individual Christians on their own growth in holiness within the context of the institutional Church's structures. As we know from living today, reforming the Church, loving the Church, and criticizing the Church all at the same time can be a difficult road to tread.

The Early Modern Church: Secularism vs. Faith

If Luther and the Protestants challenged the Church from within, the Enlightenment and the Scientific

Revolution, in retrospect, challenged the Church from the outside. It's not that some *philosophes* and scientists weren't believers, but rather that they were using a new set of criteria to ask questions and pursue answers. Simply put, Galileo said that the Church shouldn't be in the business of science and that science shouldn't be in the business of religion. It happened, however, that science and the Enlightenment sometimes ended up challenging the very idea of faith.

We can look at the early modern years as a series of "-isms": rationalism, secularism, materialism, capitalism, socialism, nationalism, industrialism, imperialism, and skepticism. Secularism began to compete with religion as the basis of a person's fundamental perspective or worldview. Skepticism wondered whether faith was possible at all and doubted whether faith and reason could coexist. Deism said a God did exist out there, but he wasn't very involved in our day-to-day lives. As Sir Isaac Newton (1642–1727) put it famously, God was a big watchmaker and the world a great watch that he built and wound up but that pretty much runs on its own. Humans could change the world, but God rarely intervened anymore.

Reason, human potential, and science became, ironically, something of a new religion, displacing faith as an organizing principle of society. With the promise that the world was entirely intelligible, some (but not all) *philosophes* and scientists saw religion as a useful mythology or belief system for prior "dark ages," but religion was no longer required for their enlightened age. To offer an example of the worst type of this thinking: one writer observed that, if you wanted to learn about the Eucharist, you might as well look it up in an encyclopedia under the word "cannibalism."

Not all *philosophes* were so antagonistic. John Locke (1632–1704), the English philosopher who had a great impact on the political philosophy of America's founding fathers, wrote a work called *The Reasonableness of Christianity.* Locke tried to find a way to deal with the Enlightenment and show its compatibility with the marriage of faith and reason, which had long been a part of Christian intellectual life. Locke said that people must see faith as understandable and reasonable, but that there were three types of beliefs. The first was a teaching that was contrary to reason and could not be believed, such as the idea that the sun rises in the west. The second was a teaching that was reasonable because it is ratified by experience: an example is God's love. The third was a teaching that was above or beyond reason, but that nevertheless could be believed because it was a revealed truth: the Trinity is this kind of true teaching that comes down to us via God's revelation and not our figuring it out.

On the other hand, not all *philosophes* were so measured. David Hume (1711–1776), the Scottish philosopher who represents a school of thought called empiricism, said that we should only believe what we experience firsthand. The German philosopher Immanuel Kant (1724–1804) argued against Locke by saying all teachings must be subjected rigidly to the principles of reason, logic, and scientific proof. Ludwig Feuerbach (1804–1872), the father of modern atheism—but at one time a believer and minister who ended up being thrown out of his parish by his own parishioners—knocked God completely out of the picture. He acknowledged that people believe in God, but he maintained that God almost surely does not exist. God exists only to the degree that people think God exists. Their image of God says nothing about God (it can't, since God doesn't really exist for Feuerbach) and everything about the person professing to believe. In essence, we made God in our own image and not the other way around. Feuerbach seemed to say that God theoretically could or might exist, but that even if God did exist, this God is entirely "other" and therefore unknowable.

But, like Locke, other early modern thinkers, ministers, and theologians married reason and revelation, demonstrating that Christianity and faith were not out of touch with the times. Many romantics, including John Henry Newman (1801–1890), the British convert and cardinal, held that reason can only take the human person so far. When the evidence ends, love of truth and faith continues. As the French philosopher and mathematician Blaise Pascal (1623–1662) said so poignantly, "There are reasons of the heart of which reason is not aware."[2] Likewise, Georg Hegel (1770–1831), a German philosopher, brought together the paired ideas of nature and grace—or, to put it another way, human action and divine action. Hegel knew that faith and reason, like nature and grace, had been synthesized in medieval theology, but that because of the Reformation, Catholics and Protestants had too often emphasized one aspect over another—leading to "either/or" thinking instead of a "both/and" combination. He recognized that the Enlightenment was continuing this split and, even worse, was subjugating or even eliminating ideas of religion, faith, and grace.

Hegel's ideas emphasized the fact that God is still dynamically alive and influencing human history and salvation. God hadn't simply stopped working, as some of the deists would have it, nor was it true that God wasn't in fact ever at work, which was the atheists' stand. Hegel wanted believers to steer a middle course between blind or heartfelt faith only and pure reason as well, which is a balance that many modern believers continue to try to strike.

The Modern Church: Building Bridges

It is difficult to determine the Church's biggest challenge in the modern world, since we are still living in the period we are trying to assess. Nevertheless, if only briefly, we can reflect on several items that have challenged the Church since the middle of the nineteenth century, without necessarily judging what was the biggest or worst of these challenges.

It cannot be denied that the Church continues to be faced by the Enlightenment challenges of rationalism, secularism, and—especially in the late twentieth and early twenty-first centuries—materialism. Faith continues to compete with rationalism and atheism. Some Christians (and people of all faiths, for that matter) find it hard to be taken seriously in their careers when they reveal themselves to be people of belief. In Europe, especially, it appears that the Christian heritage has fallen away from people's minds; some fail to see that throughout the entire history of Europe since the Roman Empire, Christianity glued society together. Elsewhere, other gods like drugs and alcohol have seized people's lives. A litany of statistics shows Church attendance has declined. But while this may be true in Europe and North America, it is not true in Asia, Africa, and Latin and South America.

At the same time, the Church has taken steps to demonstrate that she is not hiding behind a wall of blind, deaf, and dumb faith. Pope John Paul II, a former university professor, wrote a very important encyclical titled *Faith and Reason*. This letter puts this long-standing tension in context. *Faith and Reason* demonstrates that faith and reason need not compete, nor have they done so in Church history. He also said that evolution is compatible with the idea that God created the world, and he, of all people, certainly did not fail to embrace the media and technology to spread the Gospel. Most spectacularly, the Church has not distanced itself from facing down economic systems that challenge faith and human rights. The same pope who helped defeat Communism strongly criticized capitalism as well.

Contrary to conventional wisdom, religion is not doing poorly. The coming of the third millennium and the rise of the New Age demonstrated that religion as a cultural factor wields great strength. While these events may have illustrated some of the negatives connected with religion—one thinks of millennial cults and the somewhat pagan elements of the New Age—they nevertheless demonstrate religion's enduring attraction. Only hungry people hunt for spirituality. That hunt shows that traditional religions may not be satisfying the human hunger for God. But the hunt simultaneously demonstrates that spirituality has not been abandoned wholesale, either. It is a good, not a bad time for religion, but it means that Christianity has to find up-to-date ways to spread an ancient faith that is at the same time ever-new.

Similarly, as in past eras, during modernity the Church has had to think about its relationship with a changing world. For example, the early medieval *contemptus mundi* gave way to an evangelical embrace of the world with Francis of Assisi, as we have seen. Continuing this trend, Catholics embraced the idea of social Catholicism in the late nineteenth and twentieth centuries. Lay people especially tried to take care of the Industrial Revolution's cast-offs, to look after the poor and refugees of war, and to make sure that Christ is alive in the ghettos and among new immigrants. In its groundbreaking document *Gaudium et Spes,* Vatican II asked Catholics to embrace the world more fully. The council said that the Church lived with the world's joys and hopes, sorrows and anxieties.

Certainly the first few years of the third millennium witnessed much sorrow in the life of the Church when the stories broke, beginning in January 2002 in *The Boston Globe,* of those priests who had sexually abused minors and of their superiors, including some bishops, who had sometimes papered over the crimes and allowed the priests to continue to function. Horrific tales followed, dating back decades and reaching across the United States and to other countries. Once the Boston stories were out, victims who had hidden found the courage to speak out. Meanwhile, past accusations and crimes that had attracted little or no attention were recounted so that it seemed, for several months stretching to years, that the sex abuse story was a tidal wave.

People naturally asked, "Is this the worst challenge the Church has ever faced?" and they turned to Church history for an answer. A very even-handed Church historian, Jesuit Fr. John W. O'Malley, in the pages of *America* magazine answered that this scandal is unlike anything else in Church history. But he also noted that the scandal's uniqueness does not mean the current crisis is the worst challenge the Church has ever faced. Indeed, there is simply no way of knowing whether, two centuries from now, the sex abuse stories will show up in textbooks as a bump or a mushroom cloud. More plausibly, the story will be told as something in between those choices: as a major challenge that did not cripple the American Church, but led to changes and responses (especially, we may speculate, concerning the role of the laity, financial transparency, and the accountability of bishops) that we cannot yet see.[3]

Finally, the Church is living a critical moment in her internal life when it comes to Vatican II. Unfortunately, the Church is seen too often like a political body, with "conservatives" and "liberals" fighting for control on the edges, with an increasingly overlooked middle ground. Certainly, in the decade after Vatican II, progressive changes happened quickly and frequently without good catechesis backing them up. That was followed in the 1980s and 1990s by a pendulum swing in the other direction. Some called for a wholesale return to the Latin Mass and the "good old days" in the belief that turning back the clock would magically sweep away the Church's contemporary challenges. Some Catholics say that Vatican II was a mistake, while others claim the council's agenda has been ignored or even stymied. Once more, the big middle ground of moderation was lost.

We can look at this situation in two ways: as a quagmire or as an opportunity. We could lament that the Church is irrevocably divided against herself and leave the battles to the fringes. Alternately, we could decide that both ends of the spectrum have a hold on part of the picture, have something to teach the other end, but also have something to learn. This second way of looking at this situation—as an opportunity—should be the way to go, since history teaches that Trent faced a similar challenge. Finding the balance enabled the Church to move forward after Trent. She remembered what she taught, explained doctrine more clearly, evangelized the new worlds being discovered, cleaned up the mess of arithmetical piety, established better schools for priests and educational systems for lay people, and committed herself to doing a better job by admitting (if only quietly and to herself) that mistakes had been made.

Although the Church stumbled mightily after two centuries of achievement following Trent, especially in

Europe after the French Revolution, the Church found her feet again at Vatican II. It may be, then, that the Church's greatest challenge lies not behind her, but ahead. At the same time, it could well be true that history will allow the Church's believers to do now what they've often done in the past: find the acceptable middle way, strike the balance, and continue walking in the light of faith.

NOTES

General

All Scripture quotations come from the *New Revised Standard Version*.

All quotations from canon law come from the translations found in *New Commentary on the Code of Canon Law*, eds. John P. Beal, James A. Coriden and Thomas J. Green (New York: Paulist Press, 2000).

All quotations from the general councils are taken from Norman P. Tanner, ed. *Decrees of the Ecumenical Councils*, 2 vols. (London: Sheed & Ward and Washington D.C.: Georgetown University Press, 1990).

Chapter 1: Organization

1. Ignatius of Antioch: Boniface Ramsey, *Beginning to Read the Fathers* (New York: Paulist Press, 1985), pp. 109–10.

2. Cyprian: *De ecclesiae catholicae unitate,* 4–5; *Sententiae episcoporum, Patrologia Latina,* III, 1054.

3. Robert Bellarmine: *De controversiis,* vol. 2, book 3.

Chapter 2: The Laity

1. *Clericis laicos:* Brian Tierney, ed., *The Crisis of Church and State 1050–1300* (Toronto: University of Toronto Press, 1988), p. 175.

Chapter 3: The Papacy

1. Pope Julius I: Henry Bettenson, ed., *Documents of the Christian Church,* 2nd ed. (London: Oxford University Press, 1967), p. 79.

2. Bernard of Clairvaux: Julius Kirshner and Karl F. Morrison, *Medieval Europe* (Chicago: University of Chicago Press, 1986), p. 240.

3. Erasmus: *Praise of Folly,* sections 57–61.

4. Robert Bellarmine: *De potestate summi pontificis,* ch. 31.

5. Joseph de Maistre: *Du pape,* book 4.

Chapter 8: Religious Orders

1. Angela Merici: *New Catholic Encyclopedia,* 2nd ed. (Washington, D.C.: Catholic University of America Press, 2003), 14:347a.

2. John Hughes: Jay P. Dolan, *The American Catholic Experience: A History from Colonial Times to the Present* (Garden City, NY: Doubleday, 1985), p. 263.

Chapter 9: Other Faiths

1. Pope Gregory I: J. N. Hillgarth, ed., *Christianity and Paganism, 350–750: The Conversion of Western Europe* (Philadelphia: University of Pennsylvania Press, 1986), p. 152.

2. Bernard of Clairvaux: James Bruno Scott, trans., *The Letters of St. Bernard of Clairvaux* (London: Burns & Oates, 1953), p. 462.

3. Propagation of the Faith in Asia directive: Wolfgang Müller, et al., *The Church in the Age of Absolutism and Enlightenment,* trans. Gunther J. Holst (New York: Crossroad, 1981), p. 286.

4. October 1999 interreligious assembly: John Borelli, "Catholic-Muslim Relations," www.usccb.org/seia/borelli, accessed December 12, 2001.

Chapter 10: Challenges

1. Pope Gregory I: J. N. Hillgarth, ed., *Christianity and Paganism, 350–750: The Conversion of Western Europe* (Philadelphia: University of Pennsylvania Press, 1986), p. 152.

2. Blaise Pascal: *Pensées,* section IV.

3. John W. O'Malley: "The Scandal: A Historian's Perspective," *America* (May 27, 2002), 14–17.

FOR FURTHER READING

Now that you have a better understanding of the stages, key areas, and developments in Church history, you may wish to read further. The titles on this list treat many of the topics covered in this book during a specific historical period.

Aubert, Roger. *The Church in a Secularised Society.* London: Darton, Longman & Todd, 1978.

Bireley, Robert. *The Refashioning of Catholicism, 1450–1700.* Washington, D.C.: Catholic University of America Press, 1999.

Dolan, Jay P. *The American Catholic Experience: A History from Colonial Times to the Present.* Garden City, NY: Doubleday, 1985.

Frend, W. H. C. *The Rise of Christianity.* Philadelphia: Fortress Press, 1984.

Lindberg, Carter. *The European Reformations.* Oxford: Basil Blackwell, 1996.

Lynch, Joseph H. *The Medieval Church: A Brief History.* London: Longman, 1982.

Morris, Charles R. *American Catholic: The Saints and Sinners Who Built America's Most Powerful Church.* New York: Vintage Books, 1997.

Swanson, R. N. *Religion and Devotion in Europe, c. 1215–c. 1515.* Cambridge: Cambridge University Press, 1995.

For two more surveys, may I humbly suggest my own companion volumes:

Bellitto, Christopher M. *The General Councils: A History of the Twenty-One Church Councils from Nicaea to Vatican II.* New York: Paulist Press, 2002.

Bellitto, Christopher M. *Renewing Christianity: A History of Church Reform from Day One to Vatican II.* New York: Paulist Press, 2001.

 **CHRISTOPHER M. BELLITTO, PH.D.**, is Assistant Professor of History at Kean University in Union, New Jersey. His most recent books are the companion volumes, *The General Councils: A History of the 21 Church Councils from Nicaea to Vatican II* (Paulist Press, 2002), and *Renewing Christianity: A History of Church Reform from Day One to Vatican II* (Paulist Press, 2001). His articles have appeared in the *Catholic Historical Review*, *Church History*, *Cristianesimo nella storia*, *America*, *Commonweal*, and other journals. He is also a frequent public speaker and media commentator.

BOOKS & MEDIA

The Daughters of St. Paul operate book and media centers at the following addresses. Visit, call or write the one nearest you today, or find us on the World Wide Web, www.pauline.org.

CALIFORNIA
3908 Sepulveda Blvd, Culver City, CA 90230 — 310-397-8676
5945 Balboa Avenue, San Diego, CA 92111 — 858-565-9181
2650 Broadway Street, Redwood City, CA 94063

FLORIDA
145 S.W. 107th Avenue, Miami, FL 33174 — 305-559-6715

HAWAII
1143 Bishop Street, Honolulu, HI 96813 — 808-521-2731
Neighbor Islands call: — 866-521-2731

ILLINOIS
172 North Michigan Avenue, Chicago, IL 60601 — 312-346-4228

LOUISIANA
4403 Veterans Memorial Blvd, Metairie, LA 70006 — 504-887-7631

MASSACHUSETTS
885 Providence Hwy, Dedham, MA 02026 — 781-326-5385

MISSOURI
9804 Watson Road, St. Louis, MO 63126 — 314-965-3512

NEW JERSEY
561 U.S. Route 1, Wick Plaza, Edison, NJ 08817 — 732-572-1200

NEW YORK
150 East 52nd Street, New York, NY 10022 — 212-754-1110

PENNSYLVANIA
9171-A Roosevelt Blvd, Philadelphia, PA 19114 — 215-676-9494

SOUTH CAROLINA
243 King Street, Charleston, SC 29401 — 843-577-0175

TENNESSEE
4811 Poplar Avenue, Memphis, TN 38117 — 901-761-2987

TEXAS
114 Main Plaza, San Antonio, TX 78205 — 210-224-8101

VIRGINIA
1025 King Street, Alexandria, VA 22314 — 703-549-3806

CANADA
3022 Dufferin Street, Toronto, ON M6B 3T5 — 416-781-9131

¡También somos su fuente para libros, videos y música en español!